The Confidence Plan

SARAH LITVINOFF

London Borough of Camden

301110 4504141 4	
Askews	Nov-2008
	£9.99

BBC Active, an imprint of Educational Publishers LLP, part of the
Pearson Education Group
Edinburgh Gate
Harlow
Essex CM20 2JE
England

© Sarah Litvinoff 2004

BBC logo © BBC 1996. BBC and BBC ACTIVE are trademarks of the
British Broadcasting Corporation

First published 2004
Second impression 2005
Third impression 2006
This revised edition published in 2007

The right of Sarah Litvinoff to be identified as author of this Work has
been asserted by her in accordance with the Copyright, Designs and
Patents Act, 1988.

All rights reserved. No part of this publication may be reproduced,
stored in a retrieval system or transmitted in any form or by any
means electronic, mechanical, photocopying, recording, or otherwise,
without either the prior written permission of the publishers and
copyright owners or a licence permitting restricted copying in the
United Kingdom issued by the Copyright Licensing Agency Ltd., 90
Tottenham Court Road, London W1T 4LP.

ISBN: 978-1-406-61416-9

Commissioning Editor: Emma Shackleton
Project Editor: Jeanette Payne
Designer: Kevin O'Connor
Production Controller: Man Fai Lau

Printed and bound by Ashford Colour Press Ltd, UK
The Publisher's policy is to use paper manufactured from
sustainable forests.

In memory of Thomas J. Leonard,
the 'Father of Coaching'

Contents

You *can* increase
your confidence levels.

Introduction
Understanding confidence

❏ Watch for personal traps: the hidden benefits of lack of confidence
❏ Take the confidence quiz

'If you think you can or you think you can't – you're right.'

Henry Ford

Confidence is a much-desired quality but it is difficult to measure. Since becoming a coach I haven't worked with anyone who didn't suffer from a lack of confidence to some extent. Even the most outwardly poised people are racked with self-doubt on occasion. Confidence doesn't relate to what you've achieved, but to how you feel. I approached one new client with awe, having read through her CV showing page after page about her successes. She was as bold and forthright as I expected and yet, scratching the surface, I found another woman, one who was fearful of making decisions, who felt that her impressive track record had been a fluke.

Levels of confidence fluctuate according to what is going on in your life. When I started my training to be a life coach there was one thing I was convinced of: I was a good listener. By the time we were halfway through the module on listening all my confidence had evaporated. I now believed I had never listened well and never would. As I tried to put into practice the techniques I was learning, my head was filled with the buzz of instructions and I couldn't concentrate on the person talking to me at all. That is a common experience when you are learning a new or advanced skill. I seriously considered giving up my dream to become a coach. Eventually, the techniques became automatic, my faith in my capacity to be a good listener was restored and what I had learnt increased my abilities enormously. If I'd given up I never would have experienced this. Other people's reassurance that I was a good listener wouldn't have affected my own estimation. One of the messages of this book is that you can build your confidence step by step, creating real evidence of your abilities for yourself.

For some people lack of confidence and self-esteem are so acute that therapy is the only way to tackle the problem. The people I work with, however, usually function perfectly well but are being held back on some level by confidence issues. There are a number of areas that crop up time and again:

- The work they're doing and the life they're living is not of their own design, so they can't value their achievements. They feel powerless.

- Their finances are so on the edge that they feel trapped and fearful.
- They are their own worst enemies: disliking the way they look but feeling helpless to change it.
- They have problems creating relationships or are in relationships that undermine them.
- For some people it can be a combination of issues, made worse by a lack of time to deal with them properly.

I also work with people who are much more obviously unconfident but I always find that there are some things they are good at – they cook excellently, they are demon crossword solvers, they make very good friends, they are meticulous about detail, they have fertile imaginations or green fingers, or are beloved by children – whatever it is, they usually take these positive qualities for granted and focus instead on where they believe their failings are.

The difference between the two types is that the apparently confident people pour their energies into where they feel strong and assured, compensating for the areas of low self-esteem, whereas those with low confidence focus on their negative traits. Although on the surface the confident ones seem happier and more successful than the obviously unconfident, who don't recognize their own strengths, their lives are also unbalanced.

■ Introducing the 10-Step Confidence Plan

The good news is that nearly everyone who has been prepared to work with me on these issues has become more confident. Experience shows that by making simple changes and by following my techniques you can start the process yourself today.

The 10-Step Plan focuses on the elements that will bring immediate results as well as tackling the underlying issues for a permanent increase in self-esteem and well-being.

These steps can be taken in any order but I recommend that you start with the practical actions in the first two – *Take action for immediate results* and *Increase your energy*. Time and again I've seen clients quickly break the self-punishing cycle of low confidence by concentrating on these areas alone.

The *Confidence SOS: Your emergency toolbox* at the end of the book is a set of mood-changing techniques from which you can pick and choose to give your confidence a boost whenever you need it – whether before an interview, when you have to give a speech or prior to a social occasion or first date that you are dreading.

Your workbook (page 218) is designed to help you take action. By filling it in as you go along you will be cementing your commitment to change. When you finish reading each chapter, turn to *Your workbook* and complete the exercise that relates to it. Reading gives you the theory; personalizing it by acting on what you learn starts the process of turning you into a more confident person.

First of all, it is essential to look at where your own confidence needs improving, so that you can start the process today.

▪ Confidence is an attitude of mind

Confident people believe they can succeed. They are convinced they have the ability to tackle whatever comes up and they aren't put off by setbacks. A socially confident person can go alone to a big party where they know no one and feel sure they'll have a good time. 'I get on with people,' such a person will think. 'I'm good at making conversation with strangers.' Even if it's sticky at the start, with that attitude they'll persevere and mingle easily until they find someone they enjoy talking to.

People who feel confident at work will take on a difficult new project with a sense of excitement: 'I have no idea how I'm going to do this, but I always rise to a challenge.' When they make mistakes and come up against problems, they learn and try different methods, secure in the belief that they will crack it eventually. When you truly think you can, you do.

Without confidence you think you can't – and, as Henry Ford says, you prove yourself right. You think you're hopeless with computers and a new system is installed at your office. You hesitantly try to work with it, as your inner commentary screams, 'I'll never understand this! I'm bound to make a mistake!' Indeed, you do make a mistake, confirming what you think, and you give up or turn to the office expert to sort it out for you. The pages that follow will help you to start seeing mistakes or setbacks as essential milestones along the learning curve rather than using them as an excuse for giving up and ending up feeling bad about yourself.

If you find dating a daunting prospect, perhaps because a relationship has knocked your confidence, you'll be nervous about each encounter. Your inner voice will be saying, 'They won't like me' or 'I won't be able to keep the conversation going', making you feel acutely self-conscious. A lacklustre date, or meeting someone who is obviously uninterested in taking matters further, will just confirm your fears. You may not try again. When you are unconfident life seems either black or white – you see failure or success, and if you fail you take it personally. When you are confident you are more flexible, more good-humoured and more prepared to persist.

Jackie – Learning from mistakes

Jackie was convinced she'd never learn to drive. She'd had ten lessons and panicked at each one whenever she made a silly mistake. One of her talents was knitting – she made beautiful, intricate garments – and that, she said, was easy. I asked her to think back to when she was first learning to knit. She remembered how cack-handed she'd been initially. Then we talked about her graduation from plain scarves and jumpers to the complex items she made now. She remembered many failures, difficulties she had to resolve, intense frustration at times. But she had an innate confidence that she would get there in the end, so she persisted – and now she hardly gave a thought to the magic that was happening at the end of her needles. By comparing this experience with her attitude to learning to drive, Jackie was able to see how she regarded mistakes and difficulties differently when driving – they made her feel inadequate. When she was able to transfer her attitude towards learning to knit to learning to drive, she began to improve and her confidence increased.

▨ The hidden benefits of lack of confidence

If you want to improve your confidence, the idea that there may be hidden benefits to staying as you are might seem a nonsense. Who could possibly benefit from lacking confidence?

It's important to consider this more carefully. A very few people I've worked with have not become more confident. What they have in common is a reluctance to take any of the suggested steps. They are not always aware of their own reluctance and usually have an excuse, such as lack of time or events conspiring to obstruct them. Sometimes they say straight out that they can't imagine that any of the techniques could work and so they are not even prepared to try. If you dig down a little further, you will often find that their lack of confidence serves them in some way.

The 'can't try, won't try' trap

If you don't try you can't fail. Those who are unconfident will often do anything to avoid a feeling of failure. In reality, we all fail at times on the road to success. If you continue to maintain you can't do something you are protecting yourself from the inevitable setbacks before success is fully yours. There's safety in staying in the same place. For some the excuse is that they are perfectionists: in other words, unless they can be or do the best they don't want to try.

The modesty trap

Some people cling on to their lack of confidence as a form of modesty. They are often quite open about what they see as their deficiencies, saying such things as, 'Oh, I'm no good at that!' to others as well as to themselves. They almost take pride in this type of modesty. It feels more comfortable remaining as they are: 'no good'. Taking real steps towards building confidence will mean abandoning talk such as this.

The 'poor little me' trap

This is similar to the modesty trap. Some people find that letting others know that they lack confidence brings 'strokes' in the form of a great deal of loving attention as others try to build them up. They also tend to attract people who are confident in the areas where they are not – the computer novice stays forever a novice because they can always find someone else to help them out so that they never have to change. This has obvious disadvantages.

The big-headed trap

You might think that the opposite of low confidence is over-confidence and pride. In fact, those who brag and flaunt their abilities are often the least confident underneath. People with true confidence are usually genuinely modest and often believe that there is really nothing special about themselves or their abilities.

Be truthful with yourself as you consider the hidden benefits of remaining as you are. Most people can relate to these hidden benefits at least to some extent. All change is a challenge – even good change, such as becoming more confident. Being aware that ideas like these might hold you back will enable you to question them openly.

TAKE ACTION: The confidence quiz

On a scale of 1–10, where is your confidence level now? Where do you want it to be? You are likely to find that you will score better in some areas than others. Working through the 10-Step Plan in this book will help you to improve in all of them.

You will draw energy and spirit from increasing your score where you already have some confidence, and this will help you to deal with those areas where you have less.

Use this confidence quiz to plot your confidence in the following areas:

Socially
How do you feel in social situations generally?
unconfident   0 1 2 3 4 OK 6 7 8 9 10   confident

As a friend
How confident are you in your ability to make and keep friends?
unconfident   0 1 2 3 4 OK 6 7 8 9 10   confident

As a person in your own right
How do you rate your lovableness and right to happiness?
unconfident   0 1 2 3 4 OK 6 7 8 9 10   confident

Professionally
How confident are you in the work you are doing and your promotion prospects?
unconfident   0 1 2 3 4 OK 6 7 8 9 10   confident

Physically
How good do you feel about your body and what you can do with it?
unconfident   0 1 2 3 4 OK 6 7 8 9 10   confident

How you look
How secure are you in the way you look and present yourself?
unconfident   0 1 2 3 4 OK 6 7 8 9 10   confident

Sexually
How confident are you in your ability to give and receive sexual pleasure?
unconfident   0 1 2 3 4 OK 6 7 8 9 10   confident

As a partner
How secure are you in your relationship with your partner?
unconfident   0 1 2 3 4 OK 6 7 8 9 10   confident

As a parent
How happy are you with the way you interact with your children?
unconfident   0 1 2 3 4 OK 6 7 8 9 10   confident

Intellectually
How confident do you feel about your level of intelligence?
unconfident   0 1 2 3 4 OK 6 7 8 9 10   confident

Financially
How good do you feel about your present financial situation?
unconfident   0 1 2 3 4 OK 6 7 8 9 10   confident

As a competent person
How good do you feel about your resourcefulness and ability to cope?
unconfident   0 1 2 3 4 OK 6 7 8 9 10   confident

As a talented person
How confident are you that you have one special talent?
unconfident   0 1 2 3 4 OK 6 7 8 9 10   confident

As an assertive person
How do you rate your ability to make sure your feelings are respected and taken into account?
unconfident   0 1 2 3 4 OK 6 7 8 9 10   confident

In your capacity for enjoyment
How good do you feel about your capacity for enjoying yourself?
unconfident   0 1 2 3 4 OK 6 7 8 9 10   confident

These are today's scores and you'll find that they will alter from day to day and week to week. Some days you will feel better generally and all your scores will rise. Other days something will knock your confidence and your scores will go down. If there is a particular area of low confidence that you want to work on that is not mentioned here, add it to the list and score it in the same way.

▣ Using your scores to increase your confidence

One powerful technique that you can adopt right away is to monitor your scores daily, focusing on those areas where you want to improve. Three areas are probably the most you should attempt at any one time for maximum effectiveness. What's your score in each area now? What would you like it to be ideally? What score would you settle for?

Notice the times when you're at the point you'd settle for, or higher. You may find that a curious thing happens: you could end up feeling better than you thought. This is because, almost subconsciously, you will have put more effort into this area than you otherwise would have done. When you are scoring your financial confidence, for instance, you may think twice about impulse buying. Being aware of your feelings of confidence about your looks might make you pay more attention to how you dress, and so on.

As you work through the 10-Step Plan you will be returning to these daily scores, either to choose a specific area to work on further or to check on your general progress.

Every small action taken is a success in its own right.

Step 1
Take action for immediate results

❏ Discover the power of the first action

❏ Honour your commitments to yourself

❏ Take one step at a time

❏ How to cope when you can't take action

'Success is nothing more than a few simple disciplines, practised every day; while failure is simply a few errors in judgment, repeated every day. It is the accumulative weight of our disciplines and our judgments that leads us to either fortune or failure.'

Jim Rohn

Taking action is an important first step because action leads to change. When you're lacking in confidence you often feel incapable of taking action. People who come to me with confidence problems want me to help them raise their confidence levels precisely so that they *can* take action.

The fact is that confidence and taking action are inextricably interrelated. Yes, when you are feeling confident actions flow easily because you are not worried, hesitant and fearful. It works the other way as well – taking action, even the smallest of steps, builds confidence. You develop confidence as you prove to yourself that you can act. Each action is a small victory, which contributes to the confident belief 'I can'. Not taking action over a period of time erodes confidence, even where you used to have a lot.

We'll be looking at goals and taking significant action later. This step, however, concentrates on breaking the paralysis with the simplest of actions.

When you're not confident you often don't act because the problem seems too big and scary.

Angela – First steps to weight loss

Angela was seriously overweight and felt ugly, unfit and dispirited. She knew she'd never lose weight unless she did more exercise, and she believed going to a gym was the only solution. Yet the idea terrified her. Until she developed the confidence to join a gym she saw no point in dieting. In fact, she comfort-ate because she felt such a failure. She was hoping that I could give her a massive injection of confidence so that she could walk into the gym and start the process. Instead, I suggested that she should forget about losing weight for the first month of coaching.

Angela committed to two simple actions. One was to keep a food diary. She carried a small notebook and noted down everything she ate and drank at the time she did so (not at the end of the day, when the memory plays tricks). The second thing was to aim for three five-minute periods of exercise a day, such as walking round the block at lunchtime, climbing the stairs rather than taking the lift, or jigging around to some music at the end of the day. At the end of the first week she was already excited. 'I'm finding it easier not to pig out on biscuits with my notebook sitting there,' she said. 'I have two and think, I don't want to write down "six", and I put the packet away.'

By the end of the month, without actually dieting, Angela found herself motivated to cut out much of the unhealthy stuff she was eating and drinking. By paying attention to what she was putting in her mouth she increased her awareness and stopped the mindless snacking. She'd also recognized that she had an addiction to sugar and had bought a diet book that addressed this, which she'd read about in a magazine.

It was similar with the five-minute exercises. Angela quickly felt that three a day weren't enough and she looked round for more things to do. One decision was to leave the car behind and take the bus to work. By the end of the month she was getting off one stop early to increase her walking time. 'I like thinking of new things to do,' she said. 'I was early for a train last week and instead of sitting down till it arrived I took a walk.' As it happened, she'd lost about 1kg (2lb) in that first month. It was not a huge amount but she was delighted because, as she said, 'I haven't even been trying!'

The most noticeable effect was the boost in Angela's confidence. The weight loss was only a small part of this. More important was that where she had believed herself to be hopeless – lacking in willpower and self-control – she had shown herself she was capable of taking control. As her confidence grew she was able to take even more action, and by the time we finished coaching she was well on her way to losing the excess weight. Incidentally, she never did join a gym but signed up for dancing lessons instead.

■ Getting started should be easy

At this stage – and any stage where you are hesitating to act – the first action should be the easiest. Look up the phone number for the call you have to make and write it down; that's all for today. Or get out the file you need and put it on your desk (or open a word-processed one on your screen); you don't have to start work on it. Or search the internet for dating sites and bookmark them; you don't have to click into them.

You may be wondering how such small, quick actions can help. There is something disproportionately powerful about getting started and showing yourself that you are serious. When you concentrate on the very first, easiest thing rather than the scope of what lies ahead, you find it is doable. Even if that's all you do for the day you will usually experience a huge sense of relief and a raising of your spirits. Quite often this is so instantaneous that you naturally continue and do even more than you set yourself. But that's not necessary. All that matters is that you did what you committed to.

TAKE ACTION: Three simple steps to successful action

1 Pick one area for immediate action

Look back at your scores in the confidence quiz on page 15 and decide on the area where you'd like to increase your confidence. It could be where you have your lowest score, or you might feel more comfortable choosing a middling issue. Later you might want to tackle two or more areas simultaneously, but to start the experiment it is best to concentrate on one at a time.

2 Choose an easy, non-threatening action

Early success is important when confidence building, so choose something non-threatening as your first and most powerful action. For Clarissa, who was being bullied by her soon-to-be ex-husband, it was to call her solicitor to make an appointment. For Adam, who was in a financial mess, it was to start a spending notebook (similar to Angela's food diary) to see where his money was going. Kim, who was terrified about making a speech at a sales conference, asked a friend who was a confident speaker to give her some tips.

3 Check that it is doable

If you find yourself avoiding this action, it is either still too scary or you haven't reduced it to the simplest single step. For instance, Fiona, who had to prepare a report for work, had 'write first paragraph' as her action. She kept putting this off until we worked out that before she could do this she needed to know what she was going to put in the introduction. That meant reading through the notes, and to do this she first had to download the file from the computer.

■ What's really on your mind?
Quite often you'll find that the first action involves clarifying your thoughts. Your confidence is low because you are muddled and you are worrying rather than thinking constructively.

Maggie – Creating the 'right' moment

Maggie was having a difficult time at work because she believed her boss was being unfair. As is common with someone whose confidence is low, the last thing she wanted to do was confront her boss. She didn't want to 'make it worse'. What usually happens in these circumstances is that it gets worse anyway. A common pattern is that people obsess and fume privately and become more and more sensitive to the unfair treatment so that even quite innocent things seem intolerable. Inevitably, at some point it all becomes too much. People may burst into tears, lose their temper or walk out of the job with nothing resolved. And so the excuse that they were waiting for 'the right moment' results in precisely the wrong moment because they have become so wound up that they couldn't deal with the issue calmly and sensibly.

This rang a bell with Maggie. She acknowledged that, rather than waiting until she became so angry that she would erupt and lose control, it would be better to make an appointment to talk to her boss so that she could prepare her case and handle the interview in a rational and adult way. But, she told me, she didn't know what she should say because 'there's so much'.

Before Maggie was able to take the apparent first step of fixing a time to talk to her boss she needed to sort out her thinking. She agreed to write out a list of her grievances and a list of sensible requests she could make to improve the situation. She said she would email them to me, and wanted to discuss the strategy for her interview before making the appointment. In the event I didn't hear from her for a week, by which time she'd already had the meeting with her boss and they had amicably sorted out the situation.

Maggie reported that making the list had been key. 'When I wrote down the problems, I was surprised by how few points there actually were,' she said. When she looked at her list she had found it easy to see uncontroversial suggestions she could make that would improve her feelings about work. She had made an appointment with her boss the next morning for the end of the week. 'The strangest thing was that in the three days before our meeting I felt completely different,' Maggie told me. 'I knew I had the situation in hand and it seemed to me that she was being much nicer anyway. In retrospect I can see she was actually no different but I was – nothing ruffled my feathers. It meant I found it easy to be pleasant at our meeting and she didn't have the reaction I'd feared. It was almost too easy.'

The clarifying process gave Maggie the confidence she had believed she lacked, so she hadn't needed to 'borrow' some from me before her meeting.

Getting things clear in your mind can help you if you are finding it hard to settle on your first action.

■ The power of writing things down

Make a list of anything on your mind in the area where you want to increase your confidence. This is not a to-do list, though it will probably include a fair number of actions you think you have to take. Don't try to make it sensible and ordered, just write down anything that occurs to you. You should end up with a fairly long mixture – of things to do, fears, worries and perhaps a rant or two. It may look quite daunting by the end. Don't worry. The idea is to get things off your mind and on to paper, which will be a relief in itself. The aim is to identify the first action you are going to take, and then you can throw the list away if you wish or put it in a drawer. It's also possible that, like Maggie, you might be heartened by your list, and want to refer to it again – but that's not the point.

Tamara – Small steps to a big new look

Tamara's experience is a good example. When her boyfriend dumped her after six years together her confidence was at an all-time low. She desperately wanted *a new relationship but didn't know how to start dating again, and she felt no one would want her. Part of her list read:*

Dating agencies
Internet chatrooms???
Ring Andrea and suggest clubbing
Ask Sue what happened to her friend when she put in ad
Speed dating
I've got nothing to wear!!!!
Oh God, could I ever sleep with anyone else?
Blonde streaks?
I don't think I'll ever trust a man again
Invite all single friends to dinner

When we went through her list it became clear that although Tamara felt very lonely and yearned for a partner, she was nevertheless on the rebound and not really ready to start dating again as she was feeling too hurt. Yet it was clear that there were still actions she could take that would start to build her confidence for when she was ready. She decided that her first action would be to de-junk her wardrobe and collect a bag of clothes to take to the charity shop.

■ Keep up your own momentum

With that first action usually comes a surge of well-being. You know you've started, you've taken control and are on the road to building your confidence.

The secret of turning this first action into lasting confidence is to continue the process by taking one easy action every day. The cumulative effect is so powerful that, before you know it, the actions become bigger, they take less effort, and you actually feel motivated and excited. In other words, you *are* now more confident. Being consistent is more essential than the frequency. You might decide to take just three actions during the week, or only one. More important is that you make the commitment to yourself – and keep it. In Tamara's case (see page 24) her first week went like this:

Day 1: Bagged unwanted clothes for charity shop
Day 2: Took clothes to charity shop
Day 3: Sorted out what clothes needed cleaning/mending
Day 4: Made appointment with hairdresser for cut and colour
Day 5: Rehung clothes in colour groups
Day 6: Made wish-list of new garments to buy
Day 7: Bought fashion magazines to check out what was available

None of these things was difficult to do and you might think that such simple actions could not possibly have increased Tamara's confidence. But the fact is that they did. Rather than wallowing in her misery, she was taking her femininity seriously and each small action made her feel better about herself. The cumulative impact took her further and further away from her unconfident state.

Adam – Easy actions lead to financial control

Adam, who had financial problems, had similar success to Tamara. He continued to add easy actions to his first step of keeping a spending diary. When the prospect of sorting out three years' accumulation of messy accounts seemed too daunting, he stopped the rot by carrying an envelope around in his wallet so that he could slip in the receipts for the relevant month as he paid for things. Another action was simply to label a bunch of envelopes with the months and years in the neglected period. Consistently, a day's action would be to take a handful of receipts from the plastic bag in which they were all jumbled up and sort them into the relevant envelopes. Other actions included emailing for advice on a new accountant and leaving his credit cards at home and existing on the cash budget he set himself for the week. Within a month these easy and non-threatening actions had made Adam's financial situation much clearer and his accounts more manageable. He went from believing himself to be a complete idiot with money to having a new-found confidence that financial management was a skill like any other, and that he was capable of learning it.

TAKE ACTION: Create an action plan

For an action plan to succeed, it needs to be anchored in time.

1 Decide how many actions to take in a week

Every day? Five days a week? Three days? One? The more you do, the more quickly your confidence will build. But don't give yourself a hard time. It is much better to aim for fewer actions, and to be sure to do them, than to challenge yourself too strictly and then feel that you have failed. Bear in mind that when you keep a diary of your spending or eating habits, each day that you fill it in will count as a separate action.

2 Choose the easiest next action each time

You will find that actions that would have seemed impossible at the beginning will seem a lot easier a few weeks later. Some people are motivated by writing their to-do list of future actions right at the start and then scheduling them through the weeks. But I find that many people are discouraged by such a daunting list and give up. It's far better to think one day at a time and let the next action flow from what you did today, or even to take a different tack if that feels easier. Adam would have been totally put off if he had thought that he had weeks and weeks of sorting out his accounts stretching ahead of him. He managed the process in easy stages and, in addition to his daily actions, he made relevant phone calls, checked out financial management books and challenged himself to pass a day without spending any money at all.

As your confidence and mastery grow you might have a very different idea about which actions are appropriate. If Angela had scheduled her actions early on, finding and joining a gym would have featured regularly. As it was, she eventually preferred to increase her fitness in other ways.

3 Make a contract with yourself

It is particularly powerful to choose an action and then to decide, where appropriate, when you'll do it the next day. Some people feel even more committed if they write this down and sign it.

As you get into the regular habit of taking one action at a time in an area of low confidence you'll find that confidence is not simply a feeling – it grows as you build concrete proof for yourself that you can do what you decide.

See *Immediate action plan* on page 223 of *Your workbook*.

■ Unrelated action can put you back on track

I occasionally work with clients whose confidence is so low that they resist even the easiest action. Mick was like this. He had been made redundant and an ex-colleague had offered to help him with contacts and introductions to people who might be useful in his search for a new job.

Mick – Rebuilding self-esteem

Mick would commit to making the call and would then spend all day thinking about it instead of doing it. It was the same with any simple action he chose. He sat slumped in front of daytime television, snacking and drinking beer, and feeling positively revolted with himself. His house was messy, the washing-up was stacked in his filthy kitchen and he never made his bed – indeed, he often didn't even clean his teeth, never mind wash or dress, before the afternoon. Because he knew he should be doing something about looking for work, he waited around to 'feel the urge' and he believed he shouldn't do anything else in case he missed the moment. Clearly, there was an element of depression as well as lack of confidence, but before he sought treatment for that he wanted to see if there was any way he could help himself.

We agreed that he would put his job search on hold for the time being. In fact, I banned him from doing anything about it at all. His first action was to set his alarm, get up and make his bed at once (for some reason his unmade bed bothered him more than any of the other mess). His subsequent actions were all to do with getting his flat clean and tidy, limiting his television watching, changing his eating and drinking habits and getting himself into shape. During one of our sessions he told me he'd been 'bad'. It turned out that he'd made the call to his ex-colleague that he'd been resisting. He'd been out for a run and when he returned home he looked round his clean, neat flat with a sense of pride and satisfaction. 'I felt good about myself,' he said, 'and I knew that I could talk to him in the right way.'

The good news is that raising your self-esteem in any area of your life has a knock-on effect on your confidence generally. We will examine this in more detail later, especially in Steps 2 and 3: *Increase your energy* and *Build your confidence reservoir.*

If you really can't bear to take action in the area you wish to improve then choose something else that you can take action on that will make you feel good. For me, and many of my clients, it works to concentrate on health and fitness issues or the immediate environment. An area of low confidence for me is making work phone calls to people I don't know – will they be annoyed at being interrupted, dismissive or downright rude?

Actions such as taking some exercise, cleaning and clearing my desk, or dressing up as if it were a live meeting give me a sense of control and top up my confidence at the right moment.

It can also help to get a chore that has been preying on your mind out of the way. Sew on the button, go to the supermarket, check the pressure on your tyres, reorganize your filing. Doing anything at all is better than just sitting around worrying about what you are not doing.

Some people are liberated by developing a talent. Jessica was much better able to tackle difficulties at work when she spent some time each week writing a novel, and job-seeker Patrick dealt with his confidence lows by concentrating on his photography between times.

The excitement generated by doing something you are good at or love to do takes the pressure off you because your self-esteem is no longer connected entirely to the actions you fear to take.

■ The power of choosing *not* to act

Many people find that there are some days when they can't take the action they'd agreed with themselves. There appears to be a natural rebel in all of us that suddenly asserts itself. People often tell me that at these times they feel as if they are two people – the one who wants to and the one who won't. When the one who won't wins there's an immediate drop in confidence. You start to punish yourself, often by thinking the same old things – 'I knew I wouldn't be able to. It was a fluke before. I'm hopeless. I'll never be able to do this. Everyone else has more self-control than I do', and so on. Like Mick, you often spend the whole day thinking about doing something, on and off, and feeling worse all the time. You stop yourself from getting on with anything else, either because you are waiting until you feel like it or as a form of self-punishment. The odds are that this will snowball. The next time you feel even less like taking action.

Actually, everyone goes through phases like this. What separates the confident from the less so is their attitude to it. Confident people expect setbacks and snags and they know that some days are better than others. Because of this they are good at putting things behind them, forgiving themselves and starting again. Unconfident people read it differently: they see any lack of progress or motivation as a clear sign that they haven't got what it takes.

What do the confident do? They don't waste time worrying, they move on. The trick is to take control of the non-doing and consciously decide not to do something. You might wonder how this could possibly make any difference – just try it!

> When my clients are stalled I usually suggest they give themselves a time limit, say half an hour. If at the end of that time they are no nearer taking action, they tell themselves firmly, out loud or silently, 'Right, I have decided that I will not do that today.' Instead of feeling the victim of your 'bad' side, you will have taken responsibility and in so doing you will experience an immediate sense of relief and of being in control. You are now released to do something else if you wish or nothing at all if you prefer.

It is equally powerful to take responsibility for doing absolutely nothing at all or wasting time.

Duncan – Staying in control

Duncan wanted to improve his fitness by taking an evening run. There were days when he tried to psych himself up to it but stayed at his computer, surfing the web. This made him feel bad about himself. He adopted the following strategy: if at the end of half an hour he was no nearer to setting off for a run he would 'decide' to surf the web for an hour instead.

Duncan discovered three things. Firstly, by making a conscious decision not to go running he still felt in control – he had a good feeling that he would be able to go out another time rather than feeling he was on a slippery slope. Secondly, he was able to enjoy surfing the web rather than having this pleasure corroded by his bad feelings. At the end of a surfing session he felt happy and relaxed. Finally, there were occasions when he was so relaxed because he had managed to take the pressure off himself that he was able to sign off and shut his computer down even before the hour that he had allowed himself was up, and go running after all.

This decision not to do can be even more radical.

Chloe – Choosing 'less is more'

Chloe, who works as an editor for a publishing company, was feeling overlooked as people less competent were being promoted above her. She was convinced that she needed to work harder. Every evening and at weekends she would take home piles of manuscripts. More often than not she would not get round to reading any of them, and she spent her time at home feeling rotten about herself and her career prospects. It was also compromising her relationship with her husband. She couldn't relax with him and was irritated if he wanted them to do things together when he knew she should be working.

Nervously, Chloe agreed to try and change the pattern. The first step was to stop taking work home. Instead of feeling guilty about this she decided to pamper herself – she would watch television in the evenings, have a long, luxurious bath, do her nails, have an early night with her husband or a meal out with him, read a book purely for pleasure or listen to music.

Chloe's evenings and weekends became truly restorative. She felt more alert and relaxed and that made her more energetic and focused at work. She found ways of getting some of the reading done within the working day. She still needed to do more, however, so after a week she decided to take manuscripts home on just two of her working days (but never at weekends). What surprised her was that she not only felt motivated to read them on those evenings, she found she was also getting through far more than she had when she was bringing them home every night. By this time she was feeling in control rather than swamped and this had an effect on her confidence. It was the start of a change that resulted in her getting the promotion she felt she deserved.

TAKE ACTION: What to do if you've stalled

When you find you can't take the action you have planned, there are five things you can do instead.

1 Check that your first action is the easiest first step

Is there something even easier that you can do first? For instance, rather than committing to going out for a run, Duncan would sometimes commit simply to putting on his running gear – nothing else. More often than not, having taken this first step, he felt absolutely ready to go for a run. When Chloe first started taking work home again she would put just the first chapter in her bag rather than the whole manuscript.

2 Limit your thinking time

When you feel strong resistance to taking the action, limit the time you give yourself to start. Half an hour is probably the maximum. Any longer and your internal battle with yourself is likely to make you feel miserable. Sometimes a sharp request to yourself to 'do it now!' gets you moving.

3 Respect your choice *not* to act – and let it go

If you sense that you are going to end up not doing something anyway, turn the feeling into a positive decision. This will stop you giving yourself a hard time. Say firmly to yourself, 'I am not going to take that action.' Experience the sense of relief and then stop thinking about it for that day.

4 Choose to do nothing

It is quite legitimate to do nothing, to do something just for fun, or to waste time. You are not a machine. In fact, it can be positively beneficial if you allow yourself to relax. Make a conscious decision: 'I'm just going to sit here and close my eyes', 'I'm going to watch a soap', 'I'm going to call a friend for a chat', 'I'm going to check my emails', or 'I'm going to take the whole day off'. The important thing is not whether you do or don't do something but to make a definite decision rather than drift.

This also applies to doing something that appears to be negative. After Angela (page 20) had lost a lot of weight and was sticking conscientiously to her healthy eating plan, there were times when she felt impelled to eat chocolate. In the old days this would have meant an unrestrained pig-out and a feeling that everything would now go wrong. There would be more pain than pleasure in eating the chocolate because she felt so guilty. Instead, she took responsibility: 'I'm going to eat a bar of chocolate.' All I asked was that she should do nothing else while she ate it. She was to sit down, eat the chocolate slowly and enjoy every bite, knowing that this was what she'd chosen to do but had not been compelled to do. When she did this she was perfectly satisfied after eating one bar of chocolate and had no trouble returning to her regime of healthy eating.

5 Wipe the slate clean
Decide to start afresh, knowing that you have taken responsibility for your actions and have used your time well. This might be a good time to choose the first simple action you are going to take – either right now or tomorrow.

Energy and self-confidence go hand in hand. The higher your energy levels, the more quickly you will increase in confidence.

Step 2
Increase your energy

❏ Increase your energy reservoir
❏ Believe that you're worth it
❏ Know what's undermining your confidence
❏ Look after your physical well-being

'A minute's success pays the failure of years.'

Robert Browning, Apollo and the Fates

There is a direct link between confidence and energy levels. As a quick measure of your confidence at any time, consider how energetic you feel as you contemplate taking action. Where are you insecure and unconfident? Go ahead and put yourself mentally in that situation. If you're insecure socially, imagine yourself at an event full of strangers. How would you rate your energy levels on a scale of 1–10? Precisely! Or imagine yourself giving a speech, walking into the boss's office and asking for a rise, tackling a bitchy friend who has been spreading rumours about you, saying no to someone who relies on you for help or skiing down a mountain slope if you're hopelessly uncoordinated. If it's an area of vulnerability, you'll immediately feel a drop in energy, a sinking inside. You'll usually find your posture changes, you droop a little. Lack of confidence drains your energy. Conversely, energy sparks in you when you are facing a situation where you feel in control and confident.

Less well understood is the impact low energy has on your confidence. Presented with a problem when you're feeling fresh at the start of the day you feel up to the challenge. The very same problem arriving on your desk after a heavy week when you are tired and dispirited can seem unmanageable.

Low energy doesn't just make you tired. It makes you feel low generally, less confident, unresourceful, more sensitive, with a shorter fuse. The lower your energy, the more likely you are to feel depressed. You lose your good humour and become more touchy and irritable, you are slower to learn or think laterally. Your body collapses and concertinas in on itself.

■ The body-mind connection

The messages you send to your mind have a direct impact on your body. Being in, or even imagining, a situation in which you are unable to cope makes you feel instantly less energetic and happy and it shows in your posture. Just as instant is the effect on your confidence levels and general well-being when you feel energetic and your body is poised and upright. Your brain receives the message 'I'm in control' and responds with 'can do', upbeat thoughts.

I had direct experience of this at a workshop given by Tony Robbins, an authority on peak performance. We were asked to remember a time when we were feeling really happy, exuberant and in control. You might like to try this for yourself. We were working in pairs so that we could observe each other but you can also do it on your own in front of a mirror.

Our partners were asked to note the difference in the way we held ourselves, the tilt of our heads, the expression on our faces, the tension or lack of it in our bodies. We were encouraged to notice what thoughts were going through our minds, what we said to ourselves – 'I'm excited!'; 'I'm happy!'; 'Life is wonderful!' Next we had to put ourselves back into a situation where we had been depressed and unresourceful. I found I needed to sit on a chair to do this. Again our partners looked to see the changes in our posture, how our faces altered, what happened to our eyes, as we tuned in to our inner commentary: 'I'm hopeless'; 'I can't go on like this'; 'Nobody could love me'. Finally, we experimented with what we had learnt by switching between the two moods without imagining the situation.

It was extraordinary. When I consciously put myself into a depressed slouch I started to feel down and the hopeless thoughts came unbidden to my mind. Snapping straight into exhilarated mode, jumping up, pasting a smile on my face, throwing back my shoulders and so on, I went straight from pretending to be happy and invigorated to actually feeling so, with positive thoughts running through my mind. It was profound to experience for myself that just changing my body language made me feel and think differently.

An interesting result of this came a few days after the course had ended. I was sitting at my desk finding it hard to concentrate on my work, wondering if I'd ever be able to complete the article I was writing. I'd started the day in such good spirits but after less than an hour I was feeling fed up. Suddenly it occurred to me to check how I was sitting – I was slumped in exactly the same posture I had assumed when I was trying to make myself feel depressed.

I realized that I habitually slouched at the desk and, knowing what I now knew, I could see that this could explain why work often felt such a tiring, dispiriting slog. I moved to sit erect but relaxed, raised my head from where it had fallen almost in line with my shoulders, which I straightened from their tense position hunched towards my chest, and uncrossed my legs – and at once felt a surge of energy and a lightening of my mood.

Obviously, it is helpful to know this technique and others. But it is even more useful to raise your energy levels significantly on a long-term basis. This is the underpinning of confidence.

The more natural energy you have at your disposal the more quickly you will develop your confidence. Your basic mood is happier and more positive. When your energy levels are low and you feel unconfident, this affects not only your behaviour but also your thoughts and even your memories. You see things through a dark, distorted lens. It's the '3 am' effect. Most of us have the experience of waking in the small hours and finding that our worries seem huge and rather frightening. You find yourself remembering times when things have gone wrong, and you can't imagine them going right. In the morning light the problems haven't gone away but somehow they seem less menacing and insoluble. You are more likely to be able to tune into happier memories and convince yourself all is not lost. Raised energy levels are like the morning light – they make you feel more positive, and that is a step to increased confidence.

This chapter examines the three main ways you can start to increase your energy from today. These are:

- making yourself feel good;
- tackling anything that drains your energy; and
- improving your physical well-being.

■ Release your untapped energy

What can't be achieved when you are full of energy? Your enthusiasm is high and you feel powerful; practical matters can be tackled easily and problems seem small. Even an emotional whammy doesn't knock you too far off course – you are resilient. When your energy is low the opposite is true. Routine tasks exhaust you, small problems seem like mountains and getting through the day is a struggle.

Imagine you have an energy reservoir inside you. It should be strong and unperforated. If there are any holes your energy will just drain away. You're always using energy, so the level needs to be topped up regularly. An energy audit is essential maintenance:

Where are the holes?
How can the holes be plugged?

What is the source of your own energy?

How can you add more to the energy reservoir?

Overflowing energy is never a problem: you can do more, be kinder, have resources to help other people as well as yourself.

Plugging the energy holes and topping up with more energy can and should be done simultaneously. But as I can only write about one thing at a time I'm going to start with how you can raise your energy levels by making yourself feel good. It is pleasant to discover that becoming more confident is about more than hard work!

Increasing your fitness and health is incredibly important because it makes you feel good and energetic, and it also raises your levels in the long term and sustainably. (I will be dealing with this separately later. See page 51.) The fact is that you can arrange an influx of energy straight away, however unfit you are now. Energy is manufactured inside ourselves whenever we feel good or excited. Let's assume you are feeling low in energy now. Can you imagine how you'd perk up if you checked your numbers and found you'd won the lottery? If someone offered you your dream job? If the person you most wanted to hear it from told you how much they loved and valued you?

All of us have experienced these rushes of energy that seem to come from nowhere. Can you remember forcing yourself to go out to some event when you would much rather have stayed at home and had an early night? And then what happened? You had a wonderful time, laughed a lot, received compliments on how you looked, and your weariness simply evaporated. You got home late but felt so buoyed up that it was some time before you finally went to bed.

All the things I've mentioned so far are somewhat out of your control. Many people sit around wishing that something nice would happen to make them feel better. In fact, you have the choice to create nice things for yourself, every day and throughout the day. I'm not talking about anything big, expensive or time-consuming. Each little thing that makes you feel good recharges your batteries. When you are unconfident this doesn't come naturally. If you have low self-esteem you are more likely to be hard on yourself, or even to punish rather than reward yourself. You don't feel you're worth it. You feel that you have to earn the right to be good to yourself or have fun. It seems selfish.

The other argument I hear is that only very big changes can possibly make a difference, so why bother with the small things? When I'm coaching clients, I ask them to try to create nice things for themselves for a week as an experiment. I ask you to do the same. Experience for yourself how your energy levels start to rise as you treat yourself well. When you do something good for yourself, as the advertisement says, 'because I'm worth it', you actually start to feel worth it.

TAKE ACTION: A little of what you fancy makes you feel good

What makes you feel good is unique to you. It helps to remember things that have had this effect in the past. Everything on your list is your individual power source. You might want to consider what makes you feel good under the following headings.

What do you enjoy doing purely for fun?

Some people go blank at this question, so I ask them to think back to their early childhood for clues. Nothing is too frivolous to list here. One coach told me that she'd loved 'going round and round' when she was a little girl. She experimented with a swivel chair, and whizzing round on it brought back the joyous intoxication she'd remembered. She could raise her own energy levels any time by giving herself a quick twirl. Elizabeth used to enjoy 'just being silly'. This serious, hard-working manager decided to try being silly every day, and her husband got in on the act – he would bring her little gifts from the joke shop, such as a false nose or a bubble-blowing kit. One day they inflated dozens of balloons with a pump and played with them before bursting them.

Here are some of the things my clients have put on their lists:

watching a comedy programme or film
putting on some up-tempo music and dancing along
singing
reading a magazine or book
cooking
doing crossword puzzles

playing a computer game
stroking the cat
planning a sexy weekend treat with a partner
watching the big game
going out with mates (bowling, for a meal, to a club, etc.)
test-driving a Jaguar
burning aromatherapy oils
having the remote control to yourself for the entire evening
sitting in the garden listening to the sport on a Walkman
having the television off all evening and talking to a partner
calling a good friend for a chat
getting dressed up to the nines

If you're short of ideas, ask other people what they find enjoyable, and try some of their suggestions to see if they work for you.

Who makes you feel good when you see them or talk to them?

These are usually people who are upbeat and fun, or very relaxing to be with, and usually they love you and build you up rather than put you down. Listing them helps concentrate the mind on whom you need to make time to see or chat to on the phone.

What activities do you enjoy?

Which of them makes you feel better about yourself? These are some examples from my clients:

playing tennis
going to an exhibition
walking in the park
feeding the birds or ducks
a session at the gym with time to relax with the paper afterwards
driving to the country
a day at the races
snowboard lessons on a simulator

a day by the sea
an exercise video
a hot-air balloon ride
t'ai chi
yoga
swimming
gardening
going out for a run

How do you treat or pamper yourself?

Treats are gifts to yourself or indulgences of some sort, and they make you feel more relaxed and better about yourself. Here is a selection of things that have appeared on my clients' lists:

a quiet half-hour at home after work before getting caught up in the round of family activities
loafing mindlessly for one hour
crisp, clean sheets
breakfast in bed
a luxury holiday
a weekend away with a partner, without the children
a bottle of fine wine
a selection of exotic fruits
the best Swiss chocolate
a takeaway delivered to the door
body massage
a visit to the hairdresser
a lazy, candlelit bath with music
a Turkish bath
a sauna
a facial
a manicure
a pedicure
a tanning session
hiring a cleaner to blitz the place

a new gadget, such as an electronic organizer, a camera or an MP3 player

new software

a new book or CD

something new to wear

Where do you feel there is a gap in your life that you would like to fill?

This can include classes and courses, making time for meditation or religious practice, reading something challenging, or such things as brushing up on languages or another skill. It can also include 'giving back' in a way that inspires you, such as helping a charity or becoming a school governor.

What are your talents or dreams?

Developing something you are good at is one of the most powerful ways of raising your energy levels and self-esteem, as well as reducing stress. In a busy life these activities tend to be pushed out. Sometimes it means resurrecting an old dream – to be a singer, actor, dancer, poet, cartoonist, writer – perhaps no longer as a profession but as an intensely satisfying sideline. Whether it is joining something, such as an amateur dramatics group, or making time in the week to paint at home (and having your easel set up and ready), consistent application to a talent or hobby can change your feelings of confidence at quite a deep level. When you can tell yourself you are good at something, you have a sense of proportion about other areas where you feel less competent. As you make your list, don't overlook talents you might take for granted, such as gardening, cooking or DIY. The important thing is that they should be pleasurable.

Now is a good time to fill in *My energy secrets* on page 224 of *Your workbook*.

■ What can you begin to do today?

Go through your lists and see what you can do regularly. Pick out the items you could incorporate into your day without too much trouble. These will likely be things that don't take up much time or cost any money. What can you do today, or right now? Extract from all your lists the items that you can start doing fairly easily. You can come back to some of the others later. Sometimes the items will be daily, such as personal pampering, but the activity will vary – one day a scented bath, another painting nails, and so on. Many of my clients are inspired by putting these items into an energy-creating chart and ticking them off as they do them. As one of them said, 'The ticking off is a pleasure in itself! It makes me feel good. Also, I find myself motivated to do one more thing so that I can tick it off, so it's two pleasures for the price of one.'

Look again at your lists and see which of the larger items you could do once a week. These might include an evening class, a night out with your partner, a massage, and so on. If you like working with a chart you can include a box simply labelled 'weekly treat'. Then each week you can decide which one of your treats you will be enjoying, whether it's seeing one of your life-enhancing friends, having a pampering treatment or spending an evening watching videos.

For the really big items, such as something expensive or that needs arranging, like a holiday, you can begin to make plans.

Isobel's chart looked like this:

Week one	Mon	Tue	Wed	Thur	Fri	Sat	Sun
juice fresh fruit and veg							
15 mins of yoga							
30 mins of music							
a pamper item							
weekly treat							

You can put as few or as many items as you like on your list as long as you don't make it a to-do list that would be arduous to complete. The idea is to feel better about yourself, not worse. In Isobel's case two items on her list often doubled up – she would listen to her favourite music while taking her bath, for instance.

If you make a chart like this, colour in a square every day you do one of the items on it. Then monitor how you feel about yourself. How do you feel on the days you manage to do them all? All my clients report an increase in well-being and a sense of having more available energy the more of their choices they manage to do.

■ Favour quality 'feel-good' choices

Some of your treats will be pure self-indulgence and that is good, too, from time to time. Check to see whether the things you decide to do regularly make you feel good afterwards and not just at the time. If you're struggling with your weight, for instance, your pleasure in eating chocolate or drinking fine wine might be somewhat diminished as you contemplate its effects. Indeed, when you first make your lists you are likely to find that the treats that easily occur to you are often indulgences that have caused you trouble in the past. They have usually been the temptations of the moment. By thinking harder, and listing other things, you are more able to make better quality feel-good choices.

Tessa – The search for anxiety-free treats

Tessa was very enthusiastic about the concept of energy-giving treats and informed me that she was already good at spoiling herself 'because I'm worth it'. It turned out that she would routinely buy herself things – clothes, make-up, items for the home. The problem was that Tessa was in debt, and although the retail therapy made her feel good for the moment, the consequences were adding to her anxiety. She found it quite a challenge to think of anything that didn't include spending money. Eventually, she was able to identify a few things. The most potent was painting in the evenings. She was a talented water-colourist but never made time to paint any more. It gave her intense pleasure and satisfaction – far greater than the quick fix of buying herself something.

■ Taking the guilt out of feeling good about yourself

Many people fear that doing things purely to feel good about themselves is somehow bad, and that other people might suffer in some way.

Corinne – Redefining selfishness

Corinne was particularly worried about this. Her main reason for hiring a coach was that she needed to balance her working and home lives. As an independent consultant she thought she should take every job she was offered, but she felt she was failing as a parent. She didn't have the confidence to say no to work, fearing that her clients would never use her again, but one of her daughters had behavioural problems and she needed to spend more time with her. Corinne's life was timetabled to the hilt. She was also often snappy and irritable with her husband. 'But,' she said, 'I can't worry about that as well!'

Corinne agreed to look at the concept of energy-giving treats as a favour to me but was not very enthusiastic. She had no real intention of doing anything about it as she had no spare time and it seemed like another chore. When I encouraged her to talk about it she told me how she yearned for some time alone – even half an hour for a walk to clear her head. She had been a competitive gymnast in her teens but now took no exercise at all. What she fancied was to find a jazz-dancing class and really use her body again, but this would mean even more time away from the family and the paperwork in her home office. How could she ask her similarly overworked husband to look after the children for her so that she could do something so self-indulgent?

Nevertheless, she was prepared to give it a go. We agreed that she'd negotiate with her husband: if he looked after the children while she went to a jazz-dance class she'd do the same on another evening when he went out. The half-hour walks were easier to arrange. She told her husband how important they were to her and he was rather surprised that she hadn't been doing it anyway. He was fine about her regularly popping out.

Corinne felt rather 'naughty' doing these things but they made her feel much more relaxed and energetic. Indeed, the mere fact that she had the next dance class to look forward to, and the thought that she could take herself off for a walk whenever things were getting on top of her, were enough to make her feel less tense. From her point of view, however, the way it changed her idea about 'selfishness' was more important. She was much less snappy with her husband and had more patience with her difficult daughter. Paradoxically, spending a little less time with her family, doing things that made her feel good, made her far more loving, calm and generous with them. The increase in her confidence had a knock-on effect on her work. Later she radically revised her working pattern, making more money in fewer hours, while also enhancing her reputation with her clients.

■ What is draining your energy?

When I first started my training my coach introduced me to the concept of 'tolerations'. These are life's little irritants, the often undone things that are bothering you. There are also likely to be bigger things, too: issues to do with work, people, money and, the very reason you are reading this book: confidence. Large or small, all tolerations are energy drains. You could probably recite the large ones straight away. We all know the main issues in life that are getting us down and it's fairly obvious that these drain our energy. But the unimportant ones sap energy as well.

These are the holes in your energy reservoir. It probably goes without saying that if the major issues were sorted out the resulting relief and pleasure would cause a rise in energy. What I've learnt is that tackling the minor ones – the ones you ignore because they're 'not that bad' – has a significant effect as well, often out of proportion to their size and importance. One reason is that these small things are often part of the daily fabric of your life, always there: your printer is temperamental; the back door sticks; the bulb keeps blowing in one of your lamps; there's a cracked tile in the bathroom; your pepper grinder doesn't work properly; the pile of papers for recycling is getting bigger and bigger. You may succeed in forgetting about these small things until they catch your eye or you go to use them, and then there's a burst of irritation – and it happens every day, often more than once.

Because it bothers you so regularly, dealing with something that causes even a trivial annoyance gives extraordinary relief. It's like that wonderful silence when some loud music you hate stops.

Itemizing your energy drains, large and small, means that you can start to pick them off. The energy generated by dealing with a number of minor annoyances is much more than the energy needed to do them. It also gives you the impetus you need to sort out the really tough ones. Each one tackled closes a hole through which energy drains. The more holes you close, the more energetic you will be.

List your energy drains here.

_____

_____

_____

_____

_____

Alison – Taking practical action

Alison had a list of 30 or so grievances, and she certainly didn't feel up to tackling the major items, so she chose the one that seemed to be the most trivial. It annoyed her that her husband always cut the foil off a bottle of wine with a knife that he left on the side for her to deal with. Given that they had wine every night, it was a daily irritation. Once Alison had recognized this as an energy drain she bought a corkscrew with a foil-cutter. Simple, cheap and effective. She couldn't stop giggling when she told me about it: 'I can't believe what a difference it has made!'

A list of your energy drains is different from a to-do list, which it resembles. First of all, it is not necessarily an action list. Some items might involve actions you can't take, or aren't ready to – for instance, you might be driven mad by the potholes in your street, and on a to-do list you would write 'phone the council'. It's enough simply to note your annoyance on your energy-drain list.

The other main difference is that you are acknowledging that you would feel better and more energetic if you could cross an item off, any item, no matter how small. Indeed, an energy-drain list often has different items on it to a to-do list. No to-do list of mine would have had 'the dust under the sofa' on it because it was so unimportant in the scale of things. But when I realized that whenever I was watching television my eye would be drawn to the visible line of dust on the floorboards under the sofa – thoroughly annoying me and draining my energy – I knew that taking two minutes to remove the dust was essential to my well-being and feeling of relaxation.

Recognizing what drains your energy changes your attitude to doing something about it. Rather than being a chore, it becomes a gift to yourself.

TAKE ACTION: What are you putting up with?

You don't have to know what to do about things that are bothering you – just make a note of them. Recognize that if they were resolved you would have more available energy and confidence. Some of the things you note may be quite difficult – for example, emotional or communication issues, trouble at work. Steps later in this book will help you tackle these. For now, all you have to do is get a picture of what needs to change.

To help you find the minor things as well as the major ones that are at the forefront of your mind, it can help to consider the following headings.

Home and environment

What things round the home bother you? You might want to walk through the rooms mentally or physically when you make your list. Include your wardrobe – many people find a number of energy drains in the form of shoes that need reheeling, buttons that need sewing on, clothes that need ironing or cleaning. What about your neighbourhood and neighbours?

Important people

Are there any issues to do with your partner, children, extended family or friends that are causing you irritation? Is there anyone you'd like to be in touch with but aren't? Is there someone who is giving you a hard time? A misunderstanding you wish was cleared up?

Well-being

What is it about yourself that is draining your energy? Consider your health, your fitness and your looks.

Gadgets and machinery

Here you will think about your car, and appliances around the home that you haven't already listed.

Work

Is there anything bothering you about your work – for example, your hours, status, job satisfaction, work environment, your boss or your colleagues?

Finances

What are you tolerating in this area? You can look at debt, taxes and accounts, as well as things you would like to have but can't afford.

◼ Which actions are draining your energy?

Some coaches think that when you have made your list you should put it away and not look at it again for three months. Often you'll find that some of the items have been 'magically' resolved: having acknowledged their importance to your happiness you've found the time to sort them out anyway.

There is also a relief in simply writing things down, as you may well have discovered when you can't sleep and have put on the light and made a list of what's bothering you. What was previously going round in your mind stops. It's as if some part of your brain is concerned that you'll forget something important, so the same thoughts keep returning. Writing them down is a message to yourself that you are taking them seriously and won't forget. This often allows you to drift into the sleep that has been eluding you. Writing the items on your energy-drain list has a similar effect. On the list is off your mind.

Although you might decide to take this hands-off approach to your list, I personally find it better to pick off some things daily or through the week.

◼ Shape up your action plan

You will probably find that there are a number of items you can easily handle by making a quick phone call, spending a little money, asking someone else to deal with it or doing something simple you've been putting off. Put a star by these items. These are things you can pick off without too much trouble. You might want to play a game with yourself to see how fast you can clear these items, or decide that you are going to tackle one a day or a few each week. You can add 'tackle an energy drain' to your chart.

What is guaranteed is that you'll immediately feel the difference when you start. Remember: if something is large or complicated, break it down. If you are being driven mad because the spare room has become a junk room, for instance, itemize the elements: 'piles of books to be sorted', 'boxes to be gone through', 'old fridge needs to be collected', and so on, so that you can pick the easiest action. You've started.

The unstarred items on your list will probably include things that need more money to be sorted out than you currently have. You can start a fund for these or change your budget to include them.

Some more complex issues, especially to do with other people, might have to wait until your confidence grows alongside your renewed feelings of energy. That's fine: the time will come.

See if you can rid yourself of some energy drains permanently by completing the exercise on page 225 of *Your workbook*.

■ Get in shape – the physical side of confidence

What I want to do here is reinforce the message that the fitter and healthier you are the more available confidence you have. Physical well-being and health are intimately bound up with confidence. You know yourself that when you are ill you have far less energy, and your confidence in your ability to tackle things is similarly reduced. Conversely, when you are feeling on top form your spirits are raised, your stamina is greater, you feel better about yourself and your thinking ability is improved.

This is not a medical book. If you have a serious health issue you can find the detailed information you need from your doctor and in specialist books. Neither can I give detailed advice about losing weight or serious exercise. Instead, I recommend four essentials that can improve your physical well-being, whatever your state of health and fitness: more water, healthy eating, sleep, exercise.

Replenish your energy with water

We're always hearing this these days. There are two reasons why drinking water can contribute to your energy and confidence.

Firstly, the quantity and quality of water you drink affects how you think and feel. It has been shown that thoughts and feelings become distorted when your body is dehydrated. The brain, after all, is 75 per cent water, so to be able to think clearly and to feel emotionally balanced you need plenty of water.

Secondly, drinking enough water is directly related to your stamina and energy levels. Dehydration results in you feeling weak and tired, but when your body has all the water it needs it feels more energetic and better able to cope with whatever strain is put on it.

Research carried out by G.C. Pitts with athletes at Harvard University in the USA looked at the relationship between drinking water and energy. It conclusively proved that drinking extra water (more than you think you need) reduces fatigue and stress, and increases stamina and energy. In one of the experiments a group of athletes had to walk as far as they could in very hot weather. They were able to rest at regular intervals but they weren't allowed to drink anything. After three and a half hours most of them had dropped out with exhaustion.

On another day, in the same conditions, the same athletes were tested again. They were allowed to drink as much water as they wanted and this time it was six hours before exhaustion set in. During the next part of the experiment, again in comparable conditions, the athletes had to drink more water than they wanted, in amounts decided by doctors, to replace what liquid they were losing through perspiration. Amazingly, on this occasion they kept on walking and were showing no signs of exhaustion when the researcher called time at the end of the day.

So how much water should you drink? Feeling thirsty is not a reliable guideline – in fact, by the time you feel thirsty you are usually already depleted. It has been shown that drinking enough water to quench your thirst only gives your body between half and two-thirds of what it really needs.

Your body passes about 1.5 litres (3 pints) of water a day through the kidneys and intestines. In addition you breathe out about 0.25 litres (half a pint) – see how your breath mists a mirror – and lose the same amount through your skin, even when you are not visibly sweating. The guideline, therefore, is to drink about 2 litres (4 pints) per day – more if you can, particularly when it is hot.

The purest water comes from mineral sources that are rigorously controlled. France has the most stringent regulations – look for bottles that are labelled *eau minérale naturelle* – but be aware that a lot of mineral water is poorly regulated. Indeed, in many cases plain old tap water is of a higher quality, and you can improve on this by using a good water-filter.

The best way to drink the recommended daily amount of water without noticing is to keep a large glass or bottle of water by you while you work, taking sips at regular intervals. If this is not possible then drink two glasses of water in the morning before work (you can have hot water with a slice of lemon or lime if you prefer), two between breakfast and lunch, two between lunch and mid-afternoon and then two before your evening meal. It's better not to drink while eating as water dilutes your digestive juices. Fizzy mineral water tends to make you feel full more quickly than still water, so it can be harder to drink a lot of it.

Fuel your energy with healthy food

By this I mean choosing natural, unprocessed foods and eating regular meals. A healthy diet will include a variety of fresh fruit and vegetables of all colours, meat, fish and dairy products from reliable sources (organic if possible). Wholegrains are preferable to refined foods and you should avoid anything with additives, especially salt and sugar. Try to prepare your own food from fresh ingredients rather than rely on ready meals, and cut back on caffeine and alcohol.

There is some evidence to show that the additives found in a lot of 'junk' foods, fizzy drinks and sweets cause hyperactivity, irritability and aggression in some children, and it would be optimistic to assume that these products have no effect on adults. Eating healthily gives your body the best possible fuel for maximum energy, and the nutrients it needs to repair itself and throw off illness.

If you want to lose weight, or have a medical problem that requires a special diet, you need to look even more carefully at what you are eating and take advice. However, a healthy diet is not likely to conflict with your requirements; you just need to modify it.

Eating healthily also means bringing your evening meal forward. It is better to eat earlier and at least three hours before you go to bed. This allows your digestive system to work, and also has the benefit of being good for weight loss or maintenance – food eaten near bedtime is more likely to be stored as fat. You will also sleep better.

The restorative power of sleep

Some people pride themselves on being able to operate on very little sleep, but most of us need a proper night's rest. James B. Maas, a psychology professor at Cornell University in the USA, published the findings of his research into sleep and its benefits and concluded that sleeping eight hours would be wonderful, 'although still not optimal'. He recommends nine or even ten hours, as it is between the seventh and eighth hour that we get almost an hour of REM (rapid eye movement) sleep – the dreaming time which is also when the mind repairs itself. Apparently, although REM sleep occurs about every 90 minutes, the length of time we dream gets longer on each occasion, so the less you sleep, the less time your brain has to repair itself.

Lack of REM sleep means you wake up feeling tired and it will affect your mood because, like alcohol, it diminishes your brain power. It is during sleep that essential repairs on the body and the mind are carried out. Sleep also helps our bodies to fight infection. You will have noticed that when you're ill you feel more tired – a message from your body that sleep is what you need. The immune system is better able to do its work when your energy is conserved during sleep.

If you suffer from insomnia, or your sleep is being disturbed by a young baby, these facts might annoy you – you long for more sleep, if only you could get it. Indeed, when I work with clients who are deprived of sleep it becomes the top priority. Their energy levels, their confidence, their moods are all lower. Instead of being able to move forward in their lives they are lucky to be able to stand still. The insomniacs try different methods until they find one that suits them (they usually do). The sleep-deprived parents find other ways to catch up on their sleep, during the day and at weekends, until the baby settles down and sleeps through the night.

You will increase your well-being and energy levels significantly if you aim to establish regular sleep patterns. Here are some ways that can help.

Limit caffeine: Don't drink coffee, tea or other caffeine-containing drinks less than four hours before bedtime. They stimulate you artificially, making you feel more wakeful and less tuned in to your body's need for sleep.

Limit alcohol: A small amount of alcohol can be a relaxing aid to sleep, although it's still best not to drink too close to bedtime. Too much alcohol can cause disrupted sleep or insomnia and, as it is a diuretic, you may wake up during the night because you need to go to the toilet. It also promotes snoring, which affects the quality of sleep. Snoring disturbs or interrupts the healthy phases of sleep, in which deep sleep alternates with REM dreaming sleep, so you don't receive the same benefits from sleeping.

Have a regular bedtime: You will feel better if your sleep cycle has a regular rhythm. Try to establish a routine of getting up and going to bed at the same time every day.

Soothing rituals: Just as little children wind down with a bedtime routine, you can ready yourself for sleep with an adult alternative. Working until bedtime or watching an exciting TV programme can be overstimulating. Things that work instead are:

a warm bath
something light to read
warm milk
camomile tea
calming deep breathing
relaxation exercises
meditation
gentle yoga
a soothing radio programme
relaxing music

This last technique is extremely powerful: if you put on the same gentle music each night it acts like a lullaby – a signal to your brain that it's sleep-time.

Make your bedroom an oasis: Check that your bed is comfortable. Make your room as quiet as possible. Make it a place for sleeping and resting – better not to have the TV in it, for example.

Exercise earlier: If evening exercise is something you enjoy, do it at least four hours before going to bed so you have time to wind down again or you will be overstimulated.

Get problems on to paper and off your mind: Make a list of anything that is bothering you, as discussed in the energy drains section on page 49. This usually stops you worrying about them so that you can more easily drift off to sleep.

Move your body, reinvigorate your mind

Fitness comes from using your body the way it was meant to be used. Somewhere along the way 'exercise' has become synonymous with going to the gym or an aerobics or dance class, or doing something sporty. In this case it's easy to adopt an all-or-nothing view of exercise – you are either doing something structured or nothing at all. Your fitness will grow more sustainably if you widen your view of what exercise means. Moving and using your body in more ordinary ways, which still make some demands on it, has the same benefits as going to the gym or playing a sport.

The ideal is to do something you enjoy. You are much more likely to do it regularly if it is a pleasure to you. If you are fortunate, you may well have items that exercise you on your enjoyable-activities list: swimming, dancing, kick-boxing, t'ai chi, cycling, and so on. If, like me, you are not a naturally physical person you have to be more creative – I choose to walk wherever possible, and take the stairs. I enjoy lugging home a couple of bags of shopping because I know that the weight is increasing the benefit of my walk. I count 'silly dancing' to a couple of songs as exercise.

Some people give up consistent exercising because they are bored by routine. Factor this in by introducing variety. Do different things at different times to keep your interest level high. Learn something new. It also helps to join up with others. You are more likely to go swimming if you've arranged to meet a friend and you don't want to let them down.

If you have a health problem or a disability this area might be more difficult for you. Even so, you can almost always find ways to do more. You may not want to compete in the Disability Olympics but the participants show what is possible. Ask your doctor or health support group for ideas that will suit you.

Using your body more will not only benefit you physically. It will also increase your confidence, self-esteem and self-respect. Exercising can decrease depression and relieve anxiety. The effects on stress levels are well documented. The body responds to stress in a primitive way as a physical threat, gearing itself up to fight or run away: movement is demanded. When you respond to this, stress is harmlessly released. When you do nothing, the build-up of stress hormones can make you ill. Your body doesn't distinguish between activities – whether it's fighting, running away or simply using your body in some vigorous, pleasurable way. Exercising helps to burn off the stress hormones.

■ Turning good intentions into successful action

By now you probably have some ideas about how you can raise your energy levels – where your own power source is, what is draining your energy, and steps you can take to increase your physical well-being.

This knowledge might be enough to get you moving straight into action. However, you are more likely to include these things in your life if you make a firm commitment. The two practical ways in which you can help yourself are to make a chart and use your diary.

Create a chart

Experiment for a week with a chart incorporating the feel-good items you have identified. You'll know at the end of this time whether it inspires and motivates you and whether it has made a difference to how you feel.

Terry – Charting progress

Terry, a single man of 32, is an independent website designer who works from home. Although he is very good at what he does, his confidence was low in a number of areas – he procrastinated about work and was always late with it and his finances were in a mess. Typically, he would lie around in bed until about 10am, trying to make himself get up. Once he started work he often broke off to do other things, like watching daytime television or logging on to the fantasy game he loved playing, which would sometimes keep him occupied for hours.

Because he was behind with work he often stayed at his desk till midnight and usually worked over weekends as well. Terry rarely left the house and didn't want to 'waste time' cooking healthy food – he usually sent out for a curry or pizza, which he'd eat at his desk. He existed on black coffee. He rarely saw his friends and had given up his weekly game of football in the park that he had always enjoyed.

Terry's chart

The chart Terry devised is shown opposite. His weekly treats included buying a new gadget, CD or book; going to a comedy club, an exhibition, the cinema or a restaurant; taking a trip on the London Eye; staying with friends in the country, and staying in bed till noon.

Terry found that by sticking to regular working hours, and limiting his time at the desk as well as banning distractions during the day, he was getting much more done and rarely had to work over the weekend. The surge in energy and confidence that this gave him, and the free time that he now had, made fitting in his other items easier. Drinking 2 litres (4 pints) of water meant he naturally limited his coffee intake, and the health-giving effects of cooking fresh food, which included making his own smoothies (which he loved), made him feel in control of his fitness. Going out for a walk in the middle of his working day, combined with the sheer pleasure of playing football at the weekend, continued the process. He didn't ban himself from playing the online fantasy game, but he did so for only an hour, and after he'd finished work, so he thoroughly enjoyed it rather than feeling guilty. One easy action towards sorting out his finances, and picking off an energy drain daily, meant he felt in command of his life. The result of doing these things consistently was not only a rise in well-being, energy and confidence, but he also started pitching for more work and made more money.

Every person who makes a uniquely tailored chart experiences similar effects. What happens is that many of these feel-good items become routine. It's good to keep them on the chart anyway, so that you continue to acknowledge what you are doing for your own well-being – it increases your confidence.

Week one	Mon	Tue	Wed	Thur	Fri	Sat	Sun
Daily rise at 7 am							
start work at 8 am							
drink 2 litres of water							
finish work at 4 pm							
no daytime TV							
cook instead of takeaway							
get out at midday							
1 hr online fantasy game							
tackle an energy drain							
take one action re finances							
Weekly play football							
have treat							

One client of mine kept ticking her 'no cigarettes' box long after she'd given up smoking. Keeping your charts also helps you to avoid slipping into 'disaster thinking' if you've had a bad week – leafing through the earlier ones reminds you that it's just a small backward step when put in the context of the good weeks that have gone before.

You can make your own energy-creating chart on page 226 of *Your workbook*. You might like to start with a maximum of five actions at first. Your chart should be a spur to you, not an onerous to-do list! On page 227 is your chart of weekly treats to yourself. Having something to look forward to makes you feel good.

■ Respect the appointments you make with yourself

When you see 'board meeting', 'dentist', 'solicitor' or 'dinner party' in your diary you respect it – that time is blocked out and you work around it. Things that will increase your confidence and energy are similarly important. If these involve time and planning, or a regular commitment such as a meal out, time off, a massage, a yoga class, and so on, good intentions are not as effective as writing them into your diary.

Nathalie – A workaholic's lifesaver

Nathalie was a real workaholic who needed to clear space during the evenings and on the occasional weekend to take time out and recharge her batteries. The things she wanted to do would vary, so she used to cross the time out on the page in her diary and write 'time for me' in the space. However, she routinely ignored these entries, and if work or other commitments clashed with them she would neglect the promise she had made to herself. 'Time for me' sounded too wishy-washy and selfish when set against the demands of other people who seemed to need her. I encouraged her to find another phrase, one that would strengthen her resolve to keep this time for herself when she saw it. She chose the heading 'lifesaving class'. As she explained, 'Class sounds official and not to be missed, and I know this time for me is literally lifesaving. It reminds me that it is essential to keep it clear.'

The appointments that you make with yourself may be the most important ones you ever keep.

When you focus on the things you are good at you develop your confidence.

Step 3
Build your confidence reservoir

❏ Acknowledge your strengths
❏ Begin a compliments diary
❏ Always look at the positive
❏ Commit to developing your talents

'Success is the ability to go from failure to failure
without losing your enthusiasm.'

Winston Churchill

Confidence is not a steady state – you have more of it at some times than at
others. The more you concentrate on building up your confidence – in any area
– the more easily you will be able to access it when you are challenged.

Whatever you focus your attention on grows and develops. If you focus on
your weaknesses or failings you will entrench your sense of hopelessness and
lack of confidence. When you focus instead on what you are good at, what is
valuable about yourself and where you have succeeded, you will generate good
feelings and these will expand.

Most people with confidence issues find focusing on their good points
extraordinarily hard. They have usually got into the habit of fixing on the
negative aspects of themselves and their abilities. To build your confidence you
will have to do the opposite.

Helen – The joy of life

*Helen was a timid, overweight housewife in her mid-30s. She felt she had failed
at everything she had turned her hand to, yet she had the most astonishing
ability to notice and appreciate ordinary things. She could walk to the shops and
come back bursting with insights, pleasure and lots to think about. There was
nothing so tiny that it wouldn't excite or inspire her. I learnt more from her than
she did from me. She thought I was joking when I told her she had a real talent
for appreciation. Talent? Enjoying life didn't involve any effort or hard work – so
as far as she was concerned it was a useless ability and not anything to be proud
of. Then she had to admit that friends said they enjoyed her company because
of her quirky, upbeat observations on things that passed them by. Eventually, she
learnt to value this ability and as she did so her confidence in herself improved.*

TAKE ACTION: Learn to know your strengths

This exercise is all about developing the habit of looking to see the positive
in yourself. Writing things down makes them more real, which means you

can't dismiss them easily. Most of us take for granted the things we are good at and tend to ignore them so it might take you some time to come up with your list. The 'ideas' person thinks having ideas is easy, while envying and admiring the people with follow-through. The person who is good with figures thinks theirs is an everyday skill, and focuses instead on their feelings of shyness and lack of ease with other people.

Here are some ideas to get your thinking started.

- What do other people value about you?
- What do you like about yourself?
- What are you naturally good at?
- What have you achieved?

■ What do other people value about you?

Think about what friends, family, teachers or colleagues have said in your praise. Write these comments down. This can be easier than itemizing what you think you're good at. You don't have to agree with what they say, but acknowledging the good opinions other people have of you is important. I usually ask clients to list these for me before we start working together, but some still can't resist adding their own self-deprecating comments afterwards.

These are some examples from my clients of what others value about them:

Astute, streetwise, credible, professional, pragmatic, convincing, solution provider, passionate.

People say I am very level-headed and calm, and someone who is reliable.

Good memory for details of family and friends' lives, thorough, concerned with detail, good project manager (when at the best of my performance).

Good judgment – one colleague said I was one of very few people in the company that they really trust.

From a young age I remember my mum and sisters saying, 'Put her in any company and she can talk to anyone.'

Very enthusiastic, very energetic, professional, honest.

Capable, warm, artistic.

Patient, kind, non-judgmental, calm in a crisis.

■ What do you like about yourself?

Although this is harder, persist! One client wrote, 'Ummm . . . I don't dislike myself, but I haven't an answer for this one.' Eventually, I was able to tease some answers from her but she found it acutely embarrassing.

The following clients were all hard on themselves in one way or another, but nevertheless found that they liked these things about themselves:

I like the fact that I am flexible and able to get along with most people.

I'm curious by nature, questioning, analytical. Perhaps my best asset is that I like listening and asking good questions. I like that about myself – hitting on the right question and seeing how the answer fits into everything else. I worked as a researcher for years and I loved more than anything else the way I was able to piece and fit information together, and discover how it made sense (or not).

I am generous with love, money and loyalty. I am intellectual in my speech, though also intuitive in picking things up. I have a good sense of humour and can laugh easily at myself over most things; when I find I can't, I know I have hit a blockage and try to take steps to step over it.

I am adventurous and always willing to try something new.

■ What are you naturally good at?

Everyone has certain natural abilities, and they're often things that can't be measured by schools and exams. These are usually things that have always come easily to you. Make a list of them. Here are further examples that come from other people's lists:

I have a very good memory for the details of different cars.

I am a good meat and fish cook and also cook Thai food well.

I have an instinct for what makes a good photograph.

I love talking and chatting to, and finding out about people, what they do, who they are. I can make people feel comfortable.

I'm a good driver.

I'm good at quickly understanding how to use electronic gadgets, computers and software.

I stick at things until they're finished. I never leave a job half done.

I am well-coordinated and sporty, and top of my squash league.

I have an affinity with plants, and the proverbial green fingers.

I can make people laugh.

I know how to make a home a nice place to spend time in.

◼ What have you achieved?

Again, people sometimes find this hard. If they haven't climbed Everest, been awarded a first at university or made their first million, they don't think they've achieved much. To make this list, cast your net wider. After a while, you'll develop the knack of looking at your life in a different way. After much prompting, Emma came up with this list:

two lovely children
beautiful house
genuine friends
positive feedback on my new career

Emma – Embracing life's challenges

These were wonderful and genuine achievements. In fact, I knew that Emma had achieved much more than this in her busy professional life and I was hoping she would also look beyond the conventional answers to less classic achievements. Highlighting some of these, I said that from the little that I knew of her already I'd add:

The way you handled that hostile audience and had them eating out of your hand when you had to give a talk.

Choosing a good husband totally different from your father, who you said you'd never got on with (many people inexplicably find themselves choosing more of the same), and still being married 20 years later.

The ability you've developed to laugh when things are grim – and make other people laugh – and using that ability regularly.

The guts to try new things rather than settling for the known, including giving up your good job and retraining for your new career.

Maintaining single-minded focus when a goal is important. All that weight you lost – it doesn't matter that you put some back on, it proves you have the grit to do something when you decide to.

Developing high-level ability to understand people well, and matching it with professional skill to help them change their lives.

Look at your own life in this way. List your achievements, such as exams passed and skills acquired – for example, driving, languages, learning to juggle, and so on. Include all the less obvious things as well: the great support you gave to a friend in trouble, your own fortitude during a difficult time, the carefully tended plants on your terrace that inspired your neighbours to follow suit.

These lists will serve to remind you that you are valuable and appreciated, and that you have achieved things you can be proud of. You will learn that in some ways you are more confident than you previously realized and that having achieved things in the past you have the capacity to do so again.

To continue the process I recommend starting a compliments diary, which you fill in regularly. Many unconfident people find it difficult to remember the nice things that people say to them, or the occasions when they've patted themselves on the back. I've never met anyone so forgetful of these as Molly, an extraordinary and experienced trainer and workshop leader. Her academic record is formidable; she is always learning and adding to her skills, is full of original and creative ideas, and usually scores top marks in feedback from participants and colleagues. Yet when we started working together she was crippled with self-doubt.

Molly – Collecting indisputable evidence

I began to notice that Molly took the slightest criticism to heart, and was especially harsh on herself when she fell below her own high standards. She could recite negative comments going back years and was always ready to tell me what her inadequacies were. Her memory, though, was remarkably defective when it came to compliments. Sometimes she would tell me in passing about praise she'd received or acknowledge that she was pleased with her own recent performance. Yet when I reminded her of these during periods of particularly low confidence, she would go blank. 'Really?' she'd say. 'I don't remember that!'

Even when I was able to jog her memory, it was never accurate. The person hadn't 'really' meant it, or wasn't as enthusiastic as she'd originally reported – on second thoughts she hadn't been so pleased with herself.

I encouraged her to start a compliments diary, noting down praise and achievements – what other people said, and her own evaluation when it was good. I had to remind her, 'That's one for the diary!' until it became natural to her to note them down. She soon built up a body of indisputable evidence of her own achievements and abilities, and the high value she was held in by others. Simply looking through this was enough to give her a sense of proportion when she felt her confidence slipping.

Ben, another client who started to log compliments and successes, eventually so changed his belief about himself that he went for and secured promotion.

TAKE ACTION: Start a compliments diary
Here are three ways to get you started.

1 Buy an attractive notebook
Start to note down any praise or compliments you receive: 'That was so kind of you', 'You always cheer me up', 'That report was just what was needed', 'You look great', and so on. If you're pleased with something you've done, note it here as well – a compliment from you to yourself.

2 Review the way you respond to compliments
Learn to accept compliments gracefully with a simple 'thank you'. Don't dismiss or ignore them. Firstly, it's disappointing to the person who paid you the compliment – it's like rejecting a gift if you brush it aside or argue with it. Secondly, you are reinforcing your belief that you are not deserving or worthy of praise.

3 Ask for positive feedback
This takes a little more courage: ask people who seem pleased with you to tell you why. One of the first things my own coach requested I did was to ask

four people who I knew loved and valued me what it was they appreciated about me. I found this terrifying! But it was a wonderful experience. I told them it was an exercise I had been set and started it off by telling them what I loved and appreciated about them, then asked for their comments. See for yourself how rewarding this can be. These comments can go in your notebook too. Look through your notebook regularly. When your confidence is low and your brain is playing tricks on you by only 'remembering' the negative words and forgetting the positive, you have the perfect antidote.

■ Finding the good in your day
Another way to transform your feelings of confidence is to assess the day that has passed from a positive perspective. What did you do well? 'Made them laugh at lunch, finished the invoices, invented a great salad dressing, got my highest score on the computer game.' These are things you take for granted – celebrate yourself instead.

Becky – Time for reflection
Becky stumbled on this by accident. An item on her energy-creating chart was 'Be a good person'. She knew she liked herself, and felt great when she did something she defined as 'good'. Colouring in the blob became a time of reflection and pleasure about the small things she might otherwise have quickly forgotten. She was able to celebrate such things as ringing her mother for a proper chat about nothing, being kind and respectful to a harassed waiter, letting one of her staff leave early.

Look back at your day to see what you have managed to achieve rather than focusing on what remains to be done. Most of us have sneaked an extra item on to our to-do list when we've done something that wasn't on the original one, just so that we could enjoy ticking it off. Making a list afterwards of what you have done has a similar beneficial effect, especially when your to-do list remains long. Sometimes things have cropped up or you've managed to do something that wasn't in your original plan. It is possible to get to the end of a really productive day yet feel a failure because what you accomplished did not materially shorten your to-do list, either because you did something different or what you did do took longer than planned. Listing what you have achieved allows you to recognize that you are effective and still in control.

At the end of today begin filling in *Congratulate yourself* on page 228 of *Your workbook*.

■ Discover the 'What's Better?' technique

Mark Forster, author of *How to Make Your Dreams Come True*, has a different slant on the daily listing of achievements. He explains about what he calls the 'What's Better?' technique in one of his newsletters:

> At the end of each day you spend a few moments sitting down and compiling a list of everything that's been better about the day. Not, note, what's been good about the day, but what has been better about the day. It's entirely up to you to decide what you mean by the word 'better' – don't get hung up on trying to find a precise definition. Anything that strikes you as better in any sense of the word can go on the list. Also don't get hung up on the question 'better than what?'. Better than anything you like is the answer. It might be better than yesterday; it might be better than ever; it might be better than the last time you tried; better than the worst you could imagine; better than the best you could imagine – whatever!

The point of the exercise is that it gets your mind off your problems and on to the growth points in your life. It's a well-known fact that what we focus on tends to increase. So if you focus on problems, your mind will oblige by providing plenty more problems for you to deal with.

■ Connecting with your inner self

The final, powerful way to build your confidence reservoir is to develop a skill or talent, or to learn something new. Whether it's flamenco dancing, wine tasting, bee-keeping or Chinese, choose something that naturally attracts you and that you have an aptitude for. Concentrating on doing one thing supremely well will have a knock-on effect on your general sense of confidence and self-esteem.

Madeleine – Releasing the artist within

Madeleine came for coaching in her mid-50s. She'd built a successful career in administration, which she had always loathed. She wanted to give up her job but didn't have the confidence. Her husband was always putting her down, saying that she was not very intelligent and had no talents. On top of all that was her own entrenched belief that she was too old for a career change.

Art had always been Madeleine's great love at school, but her parents had stopped her studying it because they felt it would not make for a good career. As she relived her love of art, she made the decision to enrol in a part-time art course. Most of her fellow students were half her age but that made no difference to her. It quickly became apparent that she had a real feeling for colour and form. She was tremendously excited, and her tutors gave her a lot of encouragement. This revolutionized her feelings about herself and she found a new confidence, seemingly from nowhere.

As a result, Madeleine was able to stand up to her husband and challenge him to treat her with more respect. She also renegotiated her contract at work to go part-time, and used her spare hours to design her own fabrics and patterns and make a small collection of clothes.

By the time we had finished our coaching relationship Madeleine was thoroughly enjoying the new balance of her life and was also considering whether it would be possible to make a new career from her hobby.

Developing yourself through a talent or a new-found interest won't necessarily mean a complete life change, as in Madeleine's case, but it will certainly increase the depth of your confidence reservoir.

Tune in to your instincts,
and discover what
you really want.

Step 4
Be true to yourself

❏ Discover whether you are a people-pleaser
❏ Learn to trust your instincts
❏ How to set boundaries and learn to say no
❏ It's OK to ask for help

'The heart has its reasons which reason knows nothing of.'

Blaise Pascal

Confident people value themselves and respect their own feelings and needs. In contrast, unconfident people are often out of touch with their true feelings or needs because they don't think they are important enough. The result of feeling disconnected in this way is that you may find yourself living a life that doesn't suit you, and that your relationships with other people aren't as good as they could be. You don't like saying no, and even if you know what you want you find it hard to ask for it. Asserting yourself in confrontations is nearly impossible.

People who have low confidence will tend to put others first, even when it's inappropriate. This is particularly true of women, who can spend a lot of time and energy trying to please everyone except themselves.

The subtitle of Robin Norwood's book *Women Who Love Too Much* is 'When you keep hoping and wishing he'd change'. If you're a person who pleases too much then the subtext of your life is: 'When you keep hoping and wishing you'll be appreciated'. Just as women who love too much are longing hopelessly for a change, people who please too much often end up feeling resentful and sometimes worthless. What I call 'healthy selfishness' is a much better route to winning the respect, love and appreciation you are really seeking, and developing self-respect.

Louise – Taking back control

Louise is a freelance PR. She used to give her clients her mobile number and said they could call her any time. And they did – weekends, evenings, early mornings. She could never switch her phone off because it was the same number that her family, friends, babysitters and her children's school used. She was never able to relax and felt frazzled and resentful. She thought her clients would see her as ultra-professional, but the truth was that they didn't value her time and expected her to be available whenever it suited them. In the end, though, she bought a second mobile and used one number for professional calls and the other for friends and family. At first she worried that her clients would think less of her when they found they could not contact her at all hours, and she even expected some of them to take their business elsewhere. This did not happen and she was delighted to discover that their respect for her increased as her availability was restricted. It also boosted her own self-respect, and she told me that if anyone didn't like it they were the wrong clients for her.

Joanne – Setting personal boundaries

Timid, delightful Joanne was worn down coping with an acrimonious divorce, the emotions and practical aftermath of her mother's recent death and the strain of setting herself up in a new freelance career. She was letting her soon-to-be ex-husband, her children and her siblings walk all over her because she wanted to appear civilized and reasonable.

Joanne was alarmed when we worked on setting boundaries – surely, if no one was being helpful and sympathetic now they'd hate her if she put her foot down and started to demand some attention for herself. In fact, when she did, her children and brother and sister couldn't have responded better. They hadn't appreciated how tough things had been for her before she told them, and they were grateful to know how they could help. Her daughter even said, 'You're so much more fun to be with now, Mum!' Her husband was less sympathetic. He was still unpleasant and aggressive towards her, but Joanne conceded that it was no worse than it had been before and she at least felt confident enough to stand up to him and fight for what was fair and right.

If you are a constant people-pleaser, setting boundaries and letting people know what you need can be hard. This will be partly because you're nervous of antagonizing others, but also because givers always find it hard to take. And if you're uneasy about accepting the help or loving behaviour you want, you become a martyr. You end up doing so much for so little return that resentment sets in and curdles the pleasure of the very people you are trying to please. No one enjoys being with a martyr, even when they're reaping the benefits.

■ Getting rid of 'should'
Being true to yourself firstly involves identifying what you truly want in any given situation. This means bypassing thoughts of what you 'should' want, what other

people think is best or what other people do. Usually you will find that this calls for changes — often quite minor ones, but sometimes a major shift. Recognizing that you have these desires, and that they are valid, is an important first step.

As you become comfortable with identifying your true desires, and what you want from life and people, it becomes easier to make the changes you need to make. You are more able to assert yourself and tell other people what you want. The techniques that will help you to do this are outlined later in this chapter (see page 87).

■ Knowing what's important to you

If you take the time to think about what is truly important to you, you will discover the direction you need to take.

Gaby – Let your heart rule your head

Gaby came to me for coaching because she was caught between two job offers and couldn't decide which one to take. The first job represented promotion with significantly more money, but the downside was that it would have involved a long commute to the office and a lot of extra travelling. The other one would have meant much less travelling, and it was based near to where Gaby lived, but the salary was not as much as she was currently getting, and it would have been a step down in terms of status and responsibility. It seemed that her heart had decided on the second job but her head was full of counter-arguments, so she was dithering. 'Other people would give their eye teeth for the job I've been offered,' she said. 'I've put so much effort into my career and it would be a backward step for me to take the lesser job. My career might never recover. The extra money would give our family a better standard of living.'

The fact that Gaby was torn between the two options suggested that there must have been something about the lower-paid job that appealed to her. And as she looked at what she wanted from life this became clearer. She had been married for a couple of years and was now in her mid-30s, so she felt she should be thinking about starting a family. The second job would be less stressful, and she would have time to look after herself better physically and get herself into the best possible shape before conceiving.

I asked her to write a description of her life in five years' time and how she would ideally like it to be. She wrote about having two children, dogs, a rewarding home life and involvement in the local community. She saw herself working part-time for interest and extra money, but nothing high-pressured; career issues didn't figure. This vision, which was so attractive to her, made the decision simple – she took the second job.

Paul – Do what you love best

Paul didn't have such an obvious dilemma. As the owner of a small and thriving advertising agency his main concern was how quickly he could develop his business and profits. When he looked at what he wanted from life he was pragmatic. 'I love designing and coming up with ideas, of course,' he said. 'That's why I chose this profession. I'd be as happy as Larry spending my time creating. But that's not what it's about any more. I'm the director and I have to focus on management and getting new business.'

I suggested that he shouldn't worry about the practicalities for the moment and asked him to wave a magic wand and tell me what his life would be like five years down the line. He saw himself at a creative peak, with a house in the country and a flat in town, flexibly moving between the two, generating exciting and innovative campaigns. In this vision his studio ran like clockwork and it seemed that he didn't have to do anything to generate new business.

With this insight, Paul revised his strategy for growing the company. He had been hiring people with creative skills to take over the work he loved while he took care of the essential management and selling functions, which he found a slog and uninspiring. It was up to him how the company developed, and he realized that he needed to employ people with management and selling skills so that he could concentrate on what he did best and most enjoyed.

TAKE ACTION: Choosing the future you want
Here are two steps towards discovering what you really want.

1 What is your vision for the future?
Spend some time thinking about your future. For example, how would you like your life to look in five years' time. Imagine yourself there. What

is the daily pattern of your life? Don't worry about how you could make this happen, just consider what it would take to make you happy. Writing this down will give you a sense of what needs to change in your life. You'll discover what's important to you, what success and happiness mean to you – not anyone else.

Come back to this vision regularly. Sometimes you will want to add details, at other times you might want to revise it in the light of how you are changing. Usually you will find that fundamental things hold true – what you value, what makes you feel good, even if the reality you envisage looks different from your first picture. The more detailed you make this picture the better. It will remain in your mind, steering the decisions you make and solidifying your sense of your needs and feelings.

2 Identify what you can have now

A vision of an ideal life in the future usually contains elements that are outside your immediate control. It might call for money, a special person you have yet to meet, a far-off country or a job that is currently beyond your grasp. But there are usually also elements that you could have now, even if they are only part of the picture. For instance, you might have the dream of being a famous performer. When you consider the details of this, you identify that it means you will be using your talents. And perhaps it is important that people love and respect you or you see yourself physically transformed for the better. Ask yourself the following questions:

How can I use my talents anyway?

How could I perform now, if only for myself, or a small audience of uncritical family members, or getting together with colleagues for a fun performance at the Christmas party?

How can I start getting the love and respect I need from the people already in my life?

What do I need to do to start to make myself look physically as I would wish?

Look back at the answers you gave in the confidence quiz on page 15. Which areas of low confidence are getting in the way of you making changes right now? Concentrate on these, and start by taking a daily action to increase your confidence and take you closer to your vision.

Suzy – Live the life of your dreams

Suzy, a divorcee with teenage children, had a vision that revolved around a lovely new man in her life. Her divorce had left her feeling unlovable and past it. The ideal life she designed for herself was immensely detailed: the weekends they would spend in the country, the time they would spend together on joint pleasures such as going to exhibitions, taking long walks, cooking together. She imagined the kind of man he would be – his interests, his values, his kindness, his sexiness. She saw them together at her house, in a calm, uncluttered environment, with music playing, while they chatted, laughed and showed each other plenty of affection.

The vision was so clear that she started to make certain changes in her life. She redecorated and refurnished a room to be her bolt hole at home, which corresponded with the room in her dreams. She did the kinds of things she imagined doing with her man, either alone or in the company of friends – interests she had neglected for a long time.

In fact, it was two years before she met a new man she wanted to be with – through an internet dating service – but meanwhile she'd been enjoying her life so much more.

Instead of feeling needy and discontented she had developed a routine that made her much more fulfilled, and so she felt – and was – more attractive. She was so clear about the qualities of the man she wanted to share this with that she knew very quickly that the first few men she met would not be right for more than a fling and didn't carry on seeing them.

This man, however, 'ticked most of the boxes', as she said. He was not the physical type that usually appealed to her, but so much else about him was right that she looked beyond this and soon found him very attractive. In the end she had the relationship she had only dreamt about.

Turn to *My vision* on page 229 of *Your workbook* and write a description of the life you wish for yourself.

■ Tune in to your own instincts

In common with Gaby (page 78), who found her head and heart fighting over which job to take, most unconfident people find it difficult to listen to their heart. Whatever you call it – heart, gut, instinct, a funny feeling in your bones, a funny feeling in your stomach – this is a natural, wordless, instantaneous response to what is happening in your life. Often you ignore the less pleasant feelings and the messages attached to them. Someone asks you to do something and your heart sinks but you say yes anyway.

When you tune in to your own instincts you know what you want and whether something is bothering you. This is especially important when you need to assert yourself by saying no, or making requests of people, or setting boundaries. Your vision is a long-term picture of a positive response; it gives you a feeling of things being all right with your world. That's a feeling you want more of in your life, now, and not at some point in the distant future.

Gaby became very interested in this concept. 'I don't think I've ever listened to my heart,' she said. 'I don't even know how to.'

I set her the exercise of consulting her feelings through the day on minor matters – did she feel good about this or that or was she uneasy? I asked her to notice where she felt the response in her body (in her stomach, in her case) and to put her hand there when she investigated her feelings. This was to train her to notice what her natural reactions were telling her, so that she was better able to access this inner wisdom on matters of greater importance.

Try this for yourself. We all have a store of tailor-made wisdom within us. Getting to know what you really feel is a good step on the way to aligning your life with what is best for you.

■ Why saying 'no' increases confidence

Saying 'no' is a challenge for most people with confidence issues, but particularly women. You were good at it once – when you were about two years old. Watching a toddler swell with confidence when saying 'No!' to the world will remind you how empowering it is to do this. A lifetime of saying saying 'yes' when your heart says 'no' has been undermining you ever since. If you say 'yes' when you want to say 'no' you will inevitably feel resentful. This affects your energy and your well-being.

Hannah – The art of delegating

Hannah had a demanding job which, she insisted, involved her redoing other people's work when it wasn't up to standard. She was stretched at home, finding it easier to do it all herself rather than nagging her husband and children. She was also the linchpin of two committees which, she felt, would collapse without her. Her family accused her of being irritable and no fun and she felt tired all the time.

Hannah told me that there was a third committee that was begging her to take over the role of secretary. She knew that they were disorganized and she wanted a solution that would help her take on this extra responsibility. What I felt she was really asking for was permission to say 'no'. I knew this because once upon a time I had been like her. My limited amount of spare time was taken up with committees and voluntary work. Whenever someone was needed and no one else put themselves forward, I'd hear myself saying, 'I'll do it.' Just like Hannah, I felt that no one could do the job as well as me and I kept an eye on anyone who did volunteer, ready to step in.

Before long my family relationships and friendships were suffering. I was no fun to be with, and I found myself letting people down because I didn't acknowledge that I couldn't cope until it was too late for anyone else to take over. I was so busy and tired that I caught every bug going – I was burnt out.

What I learnt the hard way is that saying 'no' saves not only your sanity and your health but also your relationships. When you are less stressed you are nicer to be around. But 'no' is hard to say, particularly when you fear it is selfish. If, like me, you've being saying 'yes' because you can't help thinking that no one else could do anything as well as you, there is another way. These days, I'll offer to spend time teaching someone else how to do the job and then let go, rather than volunteering myself.

Hannah had to say 'no' not just to the new committee but also to her own demands on herself. She had to step back at work and with her family, instead of doing it all herself. As I said to her: 'Even if you had limitless energy you wouldn't be able to solve the problems of the world or your community single-handed. By passing on your skills you'll be training up an army – and that really will be a contribution to society.'

■ When to say 'no'

At an all-day conference recently I ran a workshop on life-balancing. Most of the women there admitted they lacked energy and felt tired most of the time. It raised a hollow laugh when I talked about clearing a space for themselves, to do nothing, have fun or simply pamper themselves. 'Impossible' was the verdict. Many of the older women had expected their lives to get easier when their children grew up but they now found themselves caught between looking after ageing parents and helping out with the grandchildren, not to mention the hundred and one other things that they did to support their local communities.

'You're all too busy to make any time for yourselves?' I asked innocently. They nodded. Then I slipped in the sneaky question: 'So – how come you're here today?' They'd moved heaven and earth to clear the day, neglecting for once their usual Saturday chores and commitments. They exchanged wry smiles of recognition. The impossible had become possible because they were making time for something they perceived as 'worthy', 'sensible'; because it was a conference, after all. But 'me' time? Not allowed! The impossible becomes possible when you make time to make it happen.

You must say 'no' when:
> You're overworked already
> You're tired and stressed

You have a right to say 'no' when:
> It's something you don't want to do
> It takes away from what you do want to do
> It's thankless
> You're taken for granted and people become irritated when you don't comply

It's good to say 'no' when:
> There's something you'd much rather do
> You feel you deserve some time to yourself
> It's their problem, not yours
> Just because!

Some people can't imagine getting to this last category, of pleasing themselves, or they think it's wrong. But the extraordinary thing is that when you feel completely free to say 'no' and are prepared to put yourself first for once, two things happen. Firstly, you feel happier and more energetic, and secondly, when you do say 'yes' on another occasion, it's willingly and without resentment, and people value you more. The sad thing is, when people know they are taking advantage of you they secretly feel resentful too. It's topsy-turvy but true: they feel bad and blame you for it.

Take a moment to list where you need to put your foot down, on page 230 of *Your workbook*.

■ How to say 'no'

If you're out of practice, you should know that this is a three-stage process: identifying your feelings; saying 'no'; and standing firm.

Take time to identify your feelings

If you're used to saying 'yes' all the time you may find there is a delay between saying the word and discovering how you feel. Too late, you realize you're fed up, or exhausted at the prospect of what you've agreed to. Saying 'yes' is a hard habit to break. Until you've developed your new habit of saying 'no' straight away, you need to learn to stall.

If someone asks you to do something, don't agree immediately – buy some time. Tell them something like, 'I'll have to think about that' or 'I must look at my diary/check with my husband' and then say you will let them know later (tomorrow, or in half an hour, say). Use the time you have gained in this way to decide whether you really want to say 'yes' or 'no'.

If the person presses you for an immediate decision, say pleasantly and regretfully, 'In that case I'll have to say no.'

Two good answers to the question, 'Will you do me a favour?' are: 'It depends what it is,' and 'If I can.'

Saying 'no' – keep it simple

When you've definitely decided you don't want to take something on, be brief and direct and say something like, 'No, I'm afraid I can't', 'It's not convenient',

'I'm not available', or 'Not this time'. Don't come up with a lot of apologies or excuses – the other person will often try to find solutions to them. Above all, always be pleasant.

It's not a crime to ask and it's not a crime to say 'no'. Keep your voice firm and level, and emphasize your answer with a shake of your head. If you are saying 'no' to someone who would normally expect you to say 'yes', you can soften your response with sympathy – for example, 'I know it must be hard for you to find someone for that but I'm not available and I won't be able to help you this time.' You will probably find it easier if you start your response with the word 'no'. You will keep your resolve if it's the very first word you utter.

Standing firm

When people have come to rely on you saying 'yes', they'll try to persuade you to change your mind. Don't get drawn into a discussion or argument. Just repeat your no and arm yourself with useful phrases: 'I'm sorry, but that's how it is', 'I really can't', 'I'm not free', 'It's not possible right now', or 'I really don't want to!'

Some people won't like the change in you and may be annoyed. If it's a friend or acquaintance, consider carefully whether you really want someone in your life who is only concerned about how useful you are to them. If it's family, they'll probably need some re-educating. They will need to learn that you're not always available for babysitting or chores, for instance, but as you become happier and more relaxed they'll welcome the change.

The good news is that most of the time people won't bat an eye when you say 'no'. 'Oh, OK,' will be the usual response. And they will be far more grateful when you do say 'yes' the next time.

Saying 'no' doesn't mean being unhelpful, either. You can make suggestions, such as, 'I think so-and-so could do that', or 'Have you considered such-and-such an alternative?' You can also offer compromises where you genuinely wish to: 'Tomorrow is impossible but perhaps one day next week', 'I'm too busy now but I'll give you a call when I'm freer', and 'I'm sorry I couldn't help this time, but do ask again.'

■ Say 'no' to the non-essentials

If saying 'no' comes hard to you, practice is essential. It's more difficult if you leave it until something big comes up, or if the person you are saying 'no' to is guaranteed to pile on the pressure. The experience may shake your resolve to try again. Instead, have a bit of fun saying 'no'. It can be an unimportant 'no', but you need to realize that it's not the end of the world when you do say it – and also to experience the glorious liberation that comes from using the word.

You'll find it easiest to begin with if the request is extremely trivial and you can deal with it in a light-hearted way. For instance, say 'no' when someone asks you to turn on the light or when they want to know how much you paid for something. Say 'no' to the cold-call from a salesman and to the person in the street who asks you to fill in a questionnaire. Commit to saying 'no' to something unimportant twice every day until it feels natural.

Asking for what you want

Another area of difficulty for unconfident people is asking clearly for what you want. It is an issue that affects both men and women equally. The main difference is that unconfident men may wait a long time before asking for what they want or defining what they are unhappy with; they will then deal with the matter aggressively and blame someone. Women, on the other hand, often try to indicate what they want with hints and body language – something that would be screamingly obvious to another woman but rarely to a man – and then feel hurt that they have failed to get the message across.

Some of my male clients ask me to interpret the mysterious communications they get from the women in their lives. Women don't only drop subtle hints; they will sometimes say the complete opposite of what they really want. This is genuinely baffling to most men.

Amanda – 'You just don't care!'

Amanda felt ill when she and her husband arrived at the gym together, and she wanted to go home. She asked him for the car keys. He asked her if she was all right to drive and she said she was. She left and he stayed at the gym, but when he got home later he walked into a major row. She asked him why he hadn't insisted on driving her home, and accused him of not caring that she was feeling ill and might have had an accident.

'Pleasers' often hint at what they really want by doing for other people those things that they would like other people to do for them. But if you don't make your needs explicit you'll rarely get the treatment you want. This approach assumes – mistakenly – that we all want the same thing.

Karen – Communicating your needs

When Karen had flu she stayed in bed for a week, and during that time her husband virtually ignored her. She was very upset. 'It's so unloving,' she said. 'When he's ill I fuss around him, keep popping in to see if there's anything he wants, try to tempt him with food he might like, see what I can do to cheer him up.' That was the attention she wanted for herself. I asked her whether he appreciated what she did for him. There was a silence. 'No, actually,' she said. 'He gets exasperated and tells me to leave him alone. He likes to burrow down until he feels better.' It was at this point that she realized that she was looking after her husband in the way that would suit her, and that he was treating her as he would like to be treated himself – two loving people getting it wrong by not communicating effectively.

What are you doing, at work, or with loved ones or friends, that is going unrecognized? Be truthful with yourself: what would you like to change? How do you hope other people will respond? Write down the actions or result that would please you. Now, consider what you need to ask for directly in order to achieve that outcome.

Chloe – Charting personal successes

We have met Chloe before (see page 31). She is the book editor who used to take manuscripts home every evening and at weekends. She hoped that people would notice how conscientious and hard-working she was but instead she suffered the humiliation of seeing colleagues being promoted while she was passed over. She responded by working even harder, taking on extra commitments, arriving at the office early and leaving late. It was a strategy that backfired because no one seemed to appreciate her efforts, and she became tired and irritable. She ended up seething with resentment because she felt that everyone was taking her for granted. Things started to change when Chloe restricted herself to taking work home on just two days a week and never at weekends. She experienced a surge of energy and confidence, and was able to use her time in the office more effectively. Before long she felt she was on the road to regaining control of her career and so she decided to address the issue of her promotion prospects.

Since Chloe had brought a unique talent and a great deal of publishing experience from her previous job, I encouraged her to log her successes with the company so far. She listed all the books she had acquired that had become profitable top sellers, and all the big-name authors she had signed up. I then asked her to think about what she wanted from her bosses. She came up with the following: a full-time assistant, business trips – especially to book fairs abroad, a more senior job title and an increase in salary.

This was a daunting list and at first Chloe doubted whether she'd be able to ask for any of these improvements, never mind all of them. But she decided she had nothing to lose by trying. She started with a reasoned argument for the assistant and the company agreed. Over the next few months she prepared the way for the rest of her demands by writing a series of memos to her bosses whenever she had a concrete success she wanted noted. Whenever she came up with an idea she didn't just make the suggestion verbally at a meeting, she wrote down what she had said and circulated the proposal to her colleagues. She persuaded the company to send her to a book fair in America and when she returned she wrote a report about what she had achieved by attending. Within six months she had gained everything on her wish-list, including promotion and more money.

■ Stop hinting – start asking

Catch yourself when you start hinting at what you want. Sometimes you won't even notice that you are doing it, as the request behind what you are saying will seem plain enough to you. Ask yourself if you could put a request more directly. Here are a few examples:

'Would you like me to make you a cup of tea?'
     Hidden meaning = I'd love it if you made me a cup of tea.

'Do you feel like going to the cinema?'
  Hidden meaning = I'd like to go to the cinema. Will you come?

'I don't mind. You choose.'
  Hidden meaning = I know what I really want, but I want you to insist I
  choose.

Maybe you only recognize you've been hinting when you end up making
the cup of tea and feel resentful, or if your request has been turned down – 'No,
I don't feel like going to the cinema.' You feel as if the other person has taken
away your choice because they failed, either deliberately or inadvertently, to spot
the hidden agenda.

■ What boundaries do you need?

When someone does something (or doesn't do something) that makes you feel
bad or angry, then you know that one of your personal boundaries has been
breached. We all have boundaries, whether we acknowledge them or not, and
they are different for each individual. If you don't recognize your own boundaries,
and explain them to others, they may unwittingly do things to hurt or anger you.
An angry response from you makes the other person feel defensive and angry in
turn without addressing what should change for the future. Your boundaries are
your responsibility and no one else's.

Elsa – Learning not to let rip

*Elsa felt she was assertive because she had no trouble expressing her anger.
What she didn't do was analyze what she needed to get across apart from her
indignation. After some work on boundaries she sent me this email.*

> *'A friend of mine missed an appointment with me, and only rang at
> the last minute to say she wasn't going to make it. I looked at exactly why I was
> angry, and how much of that was fair to be angry at her about. Then I spoke to
> her about it in a neutral manner, along the lines of "I am angry with you because
> you missed your appointment with me and it makes me feel you don't respect
> what I am trying to do here. I need you to give me advance notice if it ever
> happens again." What I would have done in the past is blame her for everything*

I was feeling and say something like, "You drive me up the wall, you're totally hopeless and thoughtless and because you missed the appointment I wasn't able to do A, B and C, which I would have done if we weren't meeting. I'd made arrangements to be late for something so I could fit you in," and so on. I took responsibility for the extra irritation I'd added to the situation, and just addressed the issue that she was at fault with – letting me down at the last moment. It does work, although initially it's not a very appealing idea when you just want to let rip! I have maintained my friendship with her while telling her exactly how I feel and it's quite a powerful thing to be able to do that.'

TAKE ACTION: Seven steps to setting boundaries – and sticking to them

1 Identify the problem

What do people say, do, or not do that makes you feel bad?

2 Decide what needs to change

Be specific – instead of moaning without making constructive suggestions.

3 Construct a boundary

What will you no longer put up with? What would you like instead?

4 Choose your timing

If you wait till you're furious with someone and can't stand it any more, you're unlikely to have the will to make constructive changes. You'll also find it harder to do so effectively. Things won't get better if you don't ask, so you have nothing to lose by trying. If you present your ideas at an appropriate time, and can plan properly, you stand a good chance of presenting your ideas in a way that is acceptable. Remember: anger and aggression make people defensive, and they stop listening. Pick a calm moment or agree a time to talk. Knowing in advance when you will have the conversation allows you to work out exactly what you want to say. Also, knowing that you are going to talk about it later makes you feel calmer in the meantime.

5 Explain without anger
A good formula is: 'When you . . . (the problem), I feel . . . (keep it about yourself). I'd like to suggest . . . (what you wish them to do or stop doing).'

6 Make it stick
Ask for agreement or for other suggestions. At the end of your conversation, thank the person and sum up: 'So we've agreed . . .' and repeat what you've talked about. It's then up to you to remind them, pleasantly, if they seem to forget or cross the boundary again. Many people need reminding a few times before the fact that there is a boundary sinks in, partly because they assume that what you said merely reflected the mood of the moment and they haven't yet realized how serious you are.

7 Reinforce boundaries
Take note when people do as you ask and appear to have taken your feelings into account. Let them know how pleased you are, and thank them. People will be much more motivated to respect you and your boundaries if you show your appreciation.

■ Asking for help is not a weakness
When your confidence is low it's hard to ask for help. You don't feel you deserve it and you are uncomfortable when people are helpful, or you fear they will think you are weak. In fact, we all need support, and being able to ask for help when you need it is a sign of confidence and strength.

Yvonne – Learning to ask for help
Yvonne appears confident to the world. She is a well-groomed, elegant woman with a big personality, good at talking to anyone and making people laugh. But she used to be a mass of insecurities, constantly vigilant about keeping up appearances so that people wouldn't guess at what she felt inside. Shortly after we started working together she was hit by a number of disasters. Her husband lost his job and as she wasn't working their financial position became critical.

Then her mother and son fell ill, so she had to care for both of them while trying to get a job. Even though she was losing control in private, she kept up the public front.

Yvonne rang me once in tears from a remote supermarket, which she'd gone to precisely so that should she cry, nobody she knew would see her. Eventually, she had no choice but to seek help. She had to ask neighbours to help with her family, old contacts if they could put work her way, people to help with money. 'I've lost all my pride,' she said. 'I tell them how desperate things are and throw myself on their mercy.'

For Yvonne, the unexpected result was how good this made her feel. She'd expected to feel 'lower than a worm'. It was partly the wonderful response she got from people – she'd helped so many people herself in the past and they were delighted at the opportunity to return the favour – but she also experienced huge relief at not having to pretend any more. Best of all, the act of asking actually made her feel stronger.

'I know I'm not alone and that people care,' she explained. 'Nobody looks down on me – I think they're glad I'm human. When I think of the time and emotional energy I've wasted in the past by pretending, and not accepting help!' For her, this lesson was so profound that she even felt grateful to what had happened for teaching it to her.

■ Don't ask them, tell them

If you don't make the request, you will never get help. Again, notice if you are hinting rather than asking.

A common mistake is to make the request into a question when the answer has to be yes: 'Could I have Friday morning off?' It's only when the boss says no that you reveal you have a doctor's appointment.

People need to know how important your request is

People who are better than you at saying no, need to know the level of importance of your request: the difference between an optional request and one that is of critical significance. They are more likely to put themselves out for you where necessary if they understand this. If you find it hard to ask for something, you are likely to do so hesitantly even when it is important to you – 'It doesn't matter if you can't' – and when you are taken at your word you feel devastated and even more reluctant to ask another time.

Asking can be difficult because you're putting yourself in someone else's hands, and the more important the request is the more upset or rejected you may feel if the answer is no. You may want to borrow money, ask for changes at work or need someone's emotional support.

I once had an upsetting problem and needed to talk. I rang and asked a friend if I could pop round, without saying why. She said no: she wanted an evening alone in front of the TV. I felt hurt and thought she was uncaring. Weeks later I told her how distressed I'd been. 'Why didn't you tell me?' she said. 'I would have dropped everything if I'd known.'

Ask simply

Explain what you need from people as directly as possible. Time your request so that they have the opportunity to consider it carefully. Make it clear you are going to ask them for something, and check if it's a good time before launching into it. Explain simply what your request is, why you are asking and why it's important to you. The person may still say no, but will consider it more carefully if they understand the background. If they raise objections, see if you can offer possible solutions. But if the answer has to be no, don't make the other person feel bad.

If there's a specific way in which you need help, let the person know so they can really do what you want them to do.

Be prepared for a 'no' as well as a 'yes'

Everyone has a right to say 'no', just as you do. It doesn't mean they don't care or you don't matter. To become comfortable with asking for help you have to be equally comfortable with the fact that sometimes people can't or won't help. You may not like it but it will happen from time to time. Be gracious. Thank them anyway for considering your request. As you replay the conversation, check whether you emphasized its importance to you. If someone frequently turns you down, especially when they know you really need help, you need to reassess the relationship.

The practice exercise

As with saying 'no', practise asking for help. Until it becomes natural, ask three times a day, especially if it's help you don't really need. You need to become comfortable with asking for and receiving help – and getting used to the occasional 'no'. It'll also help you say 'no' yourself. Experience the warm feeling that results from connecting with people in this way and the confidence you will develop as you become free to ask.

Each time you fail
you learn something
that can take you
closer to success.

Step 5
Don't let fear get in your way

❏ Beat the worry habit

❏ Facing up to common fears

❏ Learn the golden rules of giving and taking criticism

❏ Discover what's holding you back

'Many of life's failures are people who did not realize how close they were to success when they gave up.'

Thomas Edison

Feelings of fear contribute enormously to lack of confidence. Indeed, confidence is characterized by a lack of fear, or at least the energy to 'feel the fear and do it anyway' (the title of a book by Susan Jeffers). Some fears are so intense they become phobias, which are genuinely crippling, and you will need professional help to deal with them. But generally speaking we can choose our attitude to dealing with things, and that includes our attitude to coping with fear. This might seem surprising but by the end of this chapter you will have discovered some techniques to help you choose your attitude in situations that have previously held you back.

■ Why do we worry?

Worrying is natural. It also serves a purpose. It is part of your internal alarm system, alerting you that something is wrong and needs to be put right, or that you have to be careful. Part of listening to your instincts is tuning in to what is worrying you and why, and then deciding what to do about it. But when worry gets out of hand it is paralyzing. This can happen for three reasons:

- The first is that worry becomes a habit: you look for new things to worry about as soon as other worries are solved.
- The second is that you don't identify the action you should take when you are worried about something.
- The third is believing that worrying is more 'realistic' than having an optimistic attitude.

■ The worry habit – and taking action

Some people have had the worry habit for so long that they don't feel comfortable unless there is something to worry about – although that sounds like a contradiction. When they are not worrying they feel uneasy in case they are overlooking something important. I have sometimes been astonished by a person's capacity to worry at full throttle, whatever the degree of the problem.

Vanessa – Every worry is a big worry

Vanessa had good reason to worry as she waited for the results of a test for a potentially life-threatening disease. From the moment she knew she was in the clear she began to worry, at the same pitch, about her financial situation. When that was sorted out she obsessed about her young son's weight. When he took up sport, and began to slim down and increase his fitness, she turned her attention to the damage her cat was doing to her sofa by scratching it. The point was that the distress that Vanessa felt, and the time she spent worrying about the sofa, equalled her feelings when she thought she might die – and all the other worries in between. It was as if she had a mental slot labelled 'chief worry' and when that was empty she had to find something new to fill it.

Actions dissipate tension and worry, as you will have already discovered by following the suggestions in Step 1. It doesn't matter how small the action that you take towards solving the problem is, the relief is almost as great as the final solution, particularly if you have been dragging your feet. Worrying without action increases tension, saps your energy and creates depression. Worrying undermines your health as well as your spirits.

You can monitor your fear levels about a particular issue before and after taking action on page 231 of *Your workbook.*

■ Influencing the future

Worrying is imagining what will happen in the future. By definition, your imaginings are negative – if you are worrying, it means you think the outcome will be bad in some way. But the future is always uncertain. As you don't know what will really happen, worry will always be based on conjecture.

Look back at what you have worried about in your life. It's easiest to remember the times that your worries have been justified, but I can guarantee that on many more occasions your worries turned out to be unnecessary –

nothing bad happened and sometimes the outcome was better than you could possibly have hoped. Yet for some strange reason, worriers, and even people who don't worry unduly, believe that looking to the future and expecting things to go wrong is realistic, while imagining a situation will turn out fine is childish and far-fetched. In fact, neither is realistic in the sense that no one can accurately predict the future. It usually manages to surprise us in one way or another – and that includes psychics and pundits, and experts in the weather, politics, the financial market, and so on.

But in another way, how we choose to regard the future – whether by worrying about it or assuming that it will turn out well – does have an impact on what happens, and certainly on our life now. If you worry about what's going to happen you will generally be more fearful, and more reluctant to take action or appropriate risks. You'll be on the lookout for 'evidence' that you were right to worry. You will be less happy today. On the other hand, if you look towards the future with a more optimistic view you will feel generally more energetic and positive about what is happening in your life now. You are likely to take better and more positive action to deal with potentially critical events and are more likely to spot opportunities and things to be thankful for.

■ Putting worry into perspective

Although worrying is a natural warning bell, and useful when it prompts you to take action, it has no function beyond this. Worrying should make you apply your mind to a problem so that you can sort out what to do about it, but apart from that it serves no purpose except to wear you down and make you less able to cope. If worrying makes you study harder for your exams, for instance, that's a good use for it. However, worrying after the exam, while you are waiting for the results, imagining them to be bad, and deciding they are going to have a negative impact on your career, does nothing but depress you and cannot affect the outcome one way or another at all. (Unless, of course, you turn that worry into action.)

Asking yourself the following questions will help to keep your worries in perspective.

What's your worry worth, on a scale of 1–10?

If you've developed the worry habit you probably rarely stop and check with yourself whether what's top of your worry list is worth the anxiety. Bearing in mind how detrimental worry is to your health as well as your happiness and confidence, start catching yourself now and assess whether a worry is worth the degree of attention you are giving it. Vanessa (page 99) was initially rather offended when I questioned the importance of her less serious worries. Then she cooperated by grading the things that were worrying her from 1–10 – from minor importance to total disaster – and she eventually learnt to develop a sense of proportion.

Keep reminding yourself that worrying is useful as a spur to action but helps nothing thereafter.

What's the worst thing that can happen?

We usually shy away from following our worries to a logical conclusion, and tend to wallow in a rather formless dread about them instead. Experience has taught me that however horrible the 'worst' is, confronting it, if only once, can be a relief. I've worked with people for whom the worst possible outcome is truly frightening: death, losing their home, bankruptcy, and so on. When they put their fear into words, although it still remains frightening, it loses some of its nightmare quality. In other less extreme cases they discover that the worst that could happen is not so awful or life-changing after all. In most cases, once they have formulated the worst, they stop obsessing.

Most importantly, when you confront the worst that can happen as a reality, you can start to see it in practical terms rather than as a threatening black cloud on the horizon. Then you can see the actions you would take if the worst came to the worst, or actions you should take now to help the situation. You are back in control and are doing something more useful than worrying.

Mel – Planning ahead with breast cancer

Mel was worried about her breast cancer recurring and what would happen to her children if she were to die young. Once she faced this squarely she was able to talk about the arrangements she would need to make to put her mind at rest. She also identified that for all their sakes she would want her life to be as happy as possible in the time she had left. Instead of spending that time worrying, she decided to focus on the techniques in Step 2: Increase your energy.

Mark – Facing up to the worst, with energy

Mark was worried about his business going bust and losing all he had worked for, including his house and expensive lifestyle. I asked him to imagine for a moment that this had happened. So what would he do if it all went wrong? Where before he had sounded weary and frightened he became quite animated. 'I'd do anything!' he said. 'I'm not afraid of hard work. If it got that bad I'd take any job I could and make something of it. In some ways it would be a relief to have a clean slate and start again. We could stay with my parents till I got back on my feet.' As he got in touch with these thoughts he regained his energetic thinking. If he would be able to cope when it was that bad, what couldn't he do now while he still had options? He was able to develop some radical ideas about what to do in the current situation.

What can you do instead of worrying?

Action suspends worry because you know you are taking steps to sort it out. But sometimes there is no action you can take. It might be something like waiting for some exam results, which is outside your control, or perhaps it is a worry about something that has already happened.

Even if you can't take direct action you can still take control in other areas.

TAKE ACTION: What actions can I take?

Use your worry to identify the actions you can take. The first action is to make sure that you have all the facts you need to make an informed decision. It can help to make a list to order your thinking.

What's the problem?

What are the causes of the problem?

What are the possible solutions?

Think of at least 20 answers to these questions from the practical to the positively ridiculous. It's often after you've written down some silly answers that your brain pops up with something unusual but doable. You might also want to ask other people for their input.

What is the best possible solution? When you find the best available solution for now, take the first action towards it.

If your worry is on behalf of someone else, follow the same procedure, concentrating on what you can do to help. Offer that help but be aware that it might not be welcome. If that's the case, accept that continuing to worry will not help.

◼ Concentrate on today

Don't let your mind wander into the future or dwell on the past. Today is all you have, and this very minute is the only moment that is under your control. What can you do to make today good, profitable and happy? Look again at Step 2: *Increase your energy*, and at Step 8: *Live confidently now*. If you are worrying about someone else, taking care of your own well-being and happiness will give you the energy to be a positive support for them rather than being a drain because you are gloomy or nagging.

Look at what's good rather than what's not

What can you be thankful for today? Look for the smallest things as well as larger good fortune. If this was your last day on Earth, you'd probably appreciate normal things most: the taste of a cup of tea, the water that comes out of a tap, a dramatic sunset. Why not make a list of everything you are grateful for? You'd be surprised at how the quality of your life will improve as you concentrate on what you appreciate – especially the ordinary things that would otherwise pass you by.

Nicola's list is particularly relevant:

I am grateful for the idea of living on a day-to-day basis. It is as if the worries of the future are not invading my happiness of the present moment. Instead of fearing to live in the present, it is a great comfort to me and is the source of my contentment.

I am grateful that we can afford for Allen to have the medical attention he is getting at the moment.

*I am grateful that I do not feel that I am alone but I am also grateful that I
am becoming more confident in my own abilities to cope.*

*Instead of yearning for a job, this week I have bèen grateful that I don't
have one, as I have been very tired and I had the opportunity to rest.*

*I am grateful that my disastrous hanging basket has perked up enough to
be in pride of place by the front door.*

Learn from your mistakes

If something is not going right for you, or you have made a mistake, what can
you learn from it? If you make this kind of thinking a habit you can turn any
situation to your advantage.

Create happiness for others

Pleasant contact with other people reflects happiness back at you. Commiserate
with the harassed shop assistant. Pay those (genuine) compliments to loved ones
and friends that you've often thought but rarely get around to saying.

Change your focus

This is a good one if you are an obsessive worrier who finds it hard to get anxious
thoughts off your mind. Break the cycle by consciously changing your focus. For
example, call a friend for a chat (not about your worry!) or pick a colour and
count how many items of that colour you can see around you.

Accept what you can't change

Have a stock of mental phrases to remind yourself not to worry, to let it go.
Useful ones include:

What will be, will be.

It happened.

You can't change other people, they can only do it for themselves.

God will take care of that. (if you're religious or spiritually inclined)

The universe will provide the answer.

One day I'll understand why this had to happen. (this is one of my favourites)

Make a 'worry date' with yourself

If you're worried about not worrying, or can't imagine yourself ever getting to a point where you can stop, it helps to arrange a time and place with yourself where you will allow yourself to worry as much as you need to. Even half an hour of concentrated worrying is enough, you will find. Then, when worries come unbidden to your mind at other times you can tell yourself, 'I'll think about that at 7.30 on Thursday evening.' You can make a note of the worries as they occur if you think you'll forget them.

Lesley – A time to grieve

Lesley found this strategy enormously helpful. She was in her early 40s and her worry was that she would never be able to have children. She had taken every action she could, and there was nothing more she could do but hope, yet the worry persisted, clouding her days. The only way she found to switch off her persistent worry was when she made herself a worry date. This precious personal time not only gave her a sense of control, it was also a time for her to grieve and cry if she felt like it.

Experiment with ways to bring calm to your thoughts

If you are religious this might include praying. Otherwise, try meditation, soothing music, yoga or t'ai chi.

■ How fear affects your confidence

Worry is at the bottom of many fears. By changing your attitude to worry, you begin to combat fear generally. Here are some of the most common fears that can affect your confidence and hold you back.

Fear of change

Fear of change is very potent, and it is particularly pernicious because good change is often feared as much as bad. This is understandable as all change causes upheaval and a certain amount of tension. For instance, marrying is quite high up in the league of stress-inducing events, and other stresses include moving house (even to a bigger and better one), winning large sums of money or being promoted. Every change brings about a period of adjustment, a time when you don't know what is going to happen and when your life feels strange to you. Many people prefer the known to the unknown, even when what they have is not making them happy.

Look after yourself
Expect to be more stressed, and to have mixed feelings, when you are faced with change. Pay more attention than usual to taking care of yourself, and use the techniques discussed in Step 2: *Increase your energy*.

TAKE ACTION: Where do you want to be?
One thing that will help you to deal with the fear of change is to concentrate on your end goal. This will dispel the uncomfortable feelings that arise on the way. Envision your life as it will be after the change has happened and make the picture as clear, concrete and detailed as you can.

Fear of failure
Fear of failure is probably the most widely acknowledged fear among people who are lacking in confidence. It is important to address this because failure is an essential stage on the way to success. Almost everything you have ever succeeded at will have been preceded by some form of failure.

Consider this story that has been doing the email rounds:

at age 22 he failed in business
at age 23 he ran for state legislature and lost
at age 24 he failed in business again
at age 26 his sweetheart died and he was broken-hearted
at age 27 he had a nervous breakdown
at age 34 he eventually regained his health, running for Congress, but was defeated
at age 39 he ran for Congress again – and lost again
at age 46 he ran for the Senate and lost his ticket
at age 47 he lost when he ran for Vice-President
at age 49 he ran for the Senate again – and was defeated again

at age 51 he ran and was elected to the office of President of the United States

His name was Abraham Lincoln.

Learning something new is usually accompanied by feelings of nervousness, lack of self-belief and high stress levels, particularly in adults. Similarly, such feelings are created when you attempt to achieve a goal or have to do something you have never done before. One of the keys to dealing with your fear of failure is to recognize that you will feel like this and it will pass.

My worst attack of the fear of failure came 12 years ago when a book I had written attracted a lot of publicity. This involved me in a number of interviews and, worst of all, having to give talks in public. I was sick with fear. Before a live radio interview I hyperventilated almost to the point of passing out. I was convinced that I would talk absolute rubbish or my mind would go blank. The talks were worse because they were longer and I was on my own. In an interview, at least someone would be asking me questions and filling in any awkward silences. To give a talk I would have to stand facing an audience of people staring at me, and if panic scrambled my thoughts there would be no one to help me. I was convinced that people would be judging me, laughing at my mistakes, or would be appalled and embarrassed by my poor speaking, or bored to tears. But there was no getting out of it, I just had to do it.

Now I'm glad I had to face this ordeal. In fact, I was so determined to beat the fear that I actively sought out other occasions to give talks or workshops until I gained experience and conquered my anxiety. Now I love giving talks and am totally relaxed about speaking in public. People find it hard to believe that I was ever nervous about it, let alone frightened out of my wits. But this didn't happen overnight. The first few talks I gave were not good, the next few were just about adequate. I had to speak in public dozens of times before I became confident that I could do it well.

There were three main things that helped me.

1 I didn't compare myself with the best

At the outset my fears were made worse when I thought of the brilliant speakers I had heard, who got up without notes and talked naturally and easily, effortlessly maintaining the interest of their audience and making them laugh. I realized that comparing myself with them was unhelpful, especially when I asked one of these speakers to give me some tips. She said she had no idea how she did it, neither could she understand my fears. So I then sought out the two or three people I knew who found public speaking difficult but managed it anyway. It wasn't too hard to imagine getting to their level and they were full of good hints on dealing with fear and techniques for structuring my talk. Then I forgot about them as well. The only yardstick I used was myself. How could I do better than last time? What had I learnt since then?

You can do the same in situations where you fear failure. If comparing yourself to the best makes you want to give up, look at people who are only one notch better than you. Recognize that everyone has their own natural pace and, as soon as possible, compete only with yourself.

2 I stopped projecting my fears onto the audience

I used to imagine my audience sitting there waiting for me to fail, thinking derisive thoughts. The breakthrough came when I remembered what I felt when I was part of an audience myself, listening to a speaker. I wanted to enjoy myself, I wanted to learn something and I wanted the speaker to be good. I realized that most people were like me – generally friendly and on the side of the speaker. Instead of seeing the faces as hostile, I imagined them cheering me on.

This is something I also teach to people who fear failing at a job interview. They see the interview panel as hanging judge and jury, looking for sins. I remind them that these people want to give the job to someone, and are hoping that the candidate will perform well and be who they are looking for.

3 I prepared thoroughly

I worked very hard on each speech before I gave it. I tried it out loud to see if it sounded natural. When I reduced it to notes with headings, I went through them again and again beforehand to check that I had the right prompts. I almost knew it off by heart, so I didn't have to worry about drying up when I was on the stage. I noted parts that worked less well when I delivered it to an audience and changed the speech accordingly for the next time.

You can do this in any situation you want to improve. For instance, before job interviews prepare thoroughly – find out about the company and work out what you want to say. Practise with someone who will pretend to be the interviewer. Regard each interview as a learning experience. What questions threw you? How will you answer them next time? What do you wish you had said or done differently? Practise again, finding ways to improve your performance.

The following exercise will help you to deal with the fear of failure.

TAKE ACTION: Learning from past mistakes

Learn from the past

Can you remember a time in the past when you managed to conquer your fear or when failure led to success? Take yourself back and relive the experience in detail. Where did your courage come from? How did you cope with failure? If you can identify the place in your body where you experienced your feelings of courage, put your hand there and re-experience them.

Harness your past experiences

If you have been able to go back to a previous experience, imagine how you will cope with a similar situation now. This will strengthen you, and new ideas will occur to you. Recognize that this empowerment is part of you – a part to which you have access if you let yourself.

See every failure as a learning experience

The only time failure is negative is when the experience makes you stop trying and you give up. Each time you fail you can take something from your failure that will bring you closer to success in the future.

Fear of rejection

Fearing rejection is similar to fear of failure and it is equally paralyzing. It especially affects your courage in relationships and in any situation where you are asking to be chosen, such as a job application. The important truth to grasp, as with failure, is that rejection is inevitable. Everyone is rejected at some time or other during their lives. Not everyone will like you and some people will positively dislike you. Other people will be preferred to you for certain jobs – indeed, it is perfectly appropriate at times that you don't get a job you're after, even if you desire it passionately. It is also essential to recognize that nobody enjoys rejection, even the most confident person. It's something we all have to learn to accept and deal with.

When I was younger, rejection was my greatest fear. Being liked mattered desperately. If it was obvious someone didn't like me I felt a failure, completely worthless and a horrible person. As time went on I acknowledged how unhealthy this was. It dawned on me that I always went to extraordinary lengths to endear myself even to people that I disliked. How could that be right? It meant that I was being false; I was allowing the whim of other people (even those I did not respect) and their views to determine my confidence and self-esteem.

Eventually, I accepted that some people would never like me and even felt almost proud of this – it showed I was being true to myself, and that my confidence was more centred and under my own control. I realized my energies were better used building on relationships that were good rather than chasing after those that would never work. Now, while I certainly prefer to be liked and am disappointed if someone I like and value doesn't return the compliment, I don't feel devastated if it happens.

The three keys to changing your attitude to rejection are:

1 Don't take it personally
Someone's reaction to you is more to do with who they are than who you are. If you click with someone, you don't automatically assume it is because you are a fabulous person: you recognize that you have things in common that unite you and make you enjoy each other's company. The reverse is also true. If someone doesn't like you it's not a sign that there is something wrong with you. It just means that you are not a good match; perhaps you remind them of someone in the past who made them feel bad.

If you are turned down for a job it does not necessarily reflect on your competence or worth. You are simply not what the company is looking for right now. In truth, the company may not be right for you, either. You will be happier in a place where your face fits better.

2 Remind yourself of your value

If you find yourself feeling hurt by rejection, don't dwell on it. Think of the people who love and esteem you; remember the times you have proved your professional worth.

3 Look for the lesson

Rejection sometimes has to do with something you've done or not done. There may be a hard lesson to learn for the future, but a useful one. Taking responsibility for your actions, making amends, or making changes, will increase your confidence. When you can learn, not just suffer, you lose your fear of rejection.

Fear of conflict

Fear of conflict can hold you back from making changes in your life, either in your close relationships or at work. Many of the communication tips in Step 4: *Be true to yourself* can help you here, especially the ones relating to saying no and setting boundaries.

Fear of guilt

Guilt is a lethal emotion that can overshadow the past and make you hesitant about the impact what you want to do will have on others in the future. Guilt about treating yourself well and putting yourself first can stop you carrying out the recommendations in Step 2: *Increase your energy*.

It is appropriate to feel guilty if you have done something wrong or harmed someone by your actions. Guilt serves its purpose if you decide never to do that particular thing again or you make amends to the person you have hurt. After that, you don't need to feel guilty any more.

Guilt is less healthy when it makes you feel bad as a form of self-punishment without your acting on this feeling to atone or make changes. Some people feel they have proved they are good people because they feel guilty and awful about themselves, but when the bad feeling wears off they repeat the same actions. In the context of confidence, guilt is frequently linked to fear of success (see page 114).

Fear of criticism

What often stops you sticking your neck out is fear of the criticism you may attract. But criticism can be good as well as bad. Consider the times you have criticized someone else. Criticizing is hard to get right because we have to be sure of our own motives. What we tell someone 'for their own good' is often a way of complaining or asserting our own superiority or opinions. The only excuse for criticizing is to help another person make a change for the better. You have to ask: 'How can I say this so that the other person is able to listen and make that change?' The golden rule is to criticize the behaviour but never the person.

This golden rule also applies to criticism aimed at you, of course. If you are oversensitive to criticism you may allow someone with the wrong motives to affect you. Instead, you need to analyze whether the criticism is valid and helpfully meant, even if it is poorly expressed. In these circumstances regard it as a gift that you can learn from. Otherwise, you must disregard it.

Corinne – Choosing her own priorities

Corinne, who had so much more energy when she began to make time for herself (page 46), found that the increase in her confidence made her reassess what she was taking on and when she should say no. Although she was a highly respected independent consultant she was under the impression that her reputation was shaky. She took all the work she was offered, convinced that if she said no her clients would never ask her again. The result was that she was harassed and overworked, and felt guilty about the time she was taking from her family, particularly her difficult daughter. She was frightened that saying no would make her appear arrogant and unprofessional, and that she would be criticized.

When Corinne finally found the courage to say no – and the courage to stick to her decision – she discovered two things. Firstly, she was able to achieve a better balance between her personal and professional commitments. Secondly, and more crucially, she realized it was nobody's business but her own why she was saying no. She used to apologize to her clients and explain precisely the personal reasons why she was turning them down, but this meant that they often tried to get her to change her mind. She would end up saying yes because she took their arguments as an implied criticism. It was only when she considered whether such criticism was justified that she became indignant. How dare people suggest that she was unprofessional and wrong to give priority to her family? Creating a happy and emotionally healthy home life, she decided, was more important than anything she could achieve with her clients.

When she genuinely came to believe this, Corinne found it easy to turn work down if she didn't want to do it. She stopped explaining her motives and simply said she was too busy. To her pleasure and surprise, her clients became keener than ever to use her services and were prepared to wait until she could fit them in. This taught her more than anything else how highly people valued her. Indeed, she put up her fees significantly and, although some people dropped away, most remained and she ended up with a long waiting list of high-paying clients. She now works fewer than half the hours she used to and is earning more than she ever did.

TAKE ACTION: Criticism Checklist

Ask yourself the following questions:

Who is criticizing you?

Is it someone whose views you value in the relevant area, whose opinions you take into account? In this case consider how the criticism can help you. If you are not sure, ask the person to expand on what they have said. Or is it someone who is routinely critical and never has a nice word to say? If that's the case, you're right to take their criticism less seriously.

Is the criticism fair?

I have to confess that my knee-jerk reaction to criticism is to feel offended and get defensive. However, I find that when I sleep on it, and think about it more coolly, I can see where it is appropriate and I am then very grateful. If it continues to rankle I ask myself if it has simply touched a nerve or if it is actually wrong. Criticism is sometimes subjective and is not always justified. Try to assess what does apply and then trust your instincts about what doesn't.

How should you react?

The worst response to criticism is defensiveness. The most useful and gracious reaction, even to unjustified criticism, is to thank the person for it. That doesn't necessarily mean you have to accept it, or will follow it up once you have thought it through, but it closes the conversation pleasantly and gives the criticizer the benefit of the doubt – the criticism may have been well meant.

Be as objective as you can. The less personally you take criticism the better. Results are what count, not hurt feelings. If the same thing was said to someone else, what would you think? What would be the result if you followed the criticism? Honesty with yourself is important here. Would you or your life be better?

Fear of success

Fear of success can hold you back as much as fear of failure, though it is harder to define this. Mark Forster has a useful method for determining whether you fear success. In his newsletter he talks about discovering whether you have any negative or 'shadow' goals that stop you wanting success.

A good example would be if we decided to have a goal to be rich. So we write out 'I want to be rich' and then write out all the reasons we want to be rich.

I want to be rich because:

> *I would be able to buy anything I wanted*
> *I could have a big house, a new car (or two), and fantastic holidays*

I would have freedom from money worries
Everyone would look up to me
I could afford to have a secretary
I would have a great sense of achievement, etc. etc.

But what happens if we turn the goal round and write its negative shadow goal 'I don't want to be rich'?

I don't want to be rich because:

People would envy me
I might lose my friends
I would need to become materialistic
I might be targeted by burglars or kidnappers
The only way I could get that sort of money is if my parents died
I don't want the responsibility, etc. etc.

We are probably completely unaware of the existence of this shadow goal until we go looking for it in this sort of way. But nevertheless it is there and it is exercising a powerful influence.

The key here is to rewrite the goal so that it doesn't have a shadow. How might we rewrite the goal to be rich? We could try something like this: 'I want to be clear of debt and have enough money to pay the bills.'

Test it by writing out its shadow: 'I don't want to be clear of debt or have enough money to pay the bills.' Obviously this is a ridiculous statement which no one in their right mind would make (in normal circumstances at least), so we can be confident that the goal doesn't have a shadow.

TAKE ACTION: Embrace success

If you suspect that fear of success is holding you back, whether it's trying something new, going for promotion or making long overdue changes in your life, write out what the negative aspects of achieving your goal might be and then look at what needs to change in your attitude. It can be helpful to look for evidence that contradicts these negatives.

Heidi – Adjusting to positive change

Heidi insisted that she was desperate to lose weight. She would lose a certain amount, stay static for a while and then start to put it all back on. She made comments about the fact that people warmed to her and found her unthreatening because she was overweight. She often spoke rather disparagingly of slim women who put other women's backs up. When she tried to find examples of slim women that other women liked and accepted as much as her she found it difficult.

Heidi wondered if she was projecting her own envy on to other people and began to notice that not everyone had the same reactions as she did. Her new awareness made her realize that it was fear of slimming success that was getting in her way and she was able to address it.

Her new goal became: 'I want to remain as approachable and friendly as I am now while having a body that is fit and toned.'

▪ Conquering fear

This is an issue you will probably want to come back to time and again. Dealing with fear is a continuing process and it can crop up at different times in your life. Consider the advice of coach Michael Neill in one of his regular email tips:

Whatever it is you're trying to achieve, ask yourself what you would do if you weren't afraid. Don't worry about whether or not you actually are or aren't afraid – just notice your answers, and notice which ones you want to act on. You may find yourself living beyond fear – and freedom is a jolly nice place to live.

Make time for people who believe in you the most – they will boost your confidence levels.

Step 6
Create energizing relationships

❏ Develop confidence-creating friendships
❏ Identify the energy vampires – moaners, crushers and critics
❏ How to be a good friend

'The only way to have a friend is to be one.'

Ralph Waldo Emerson

The aim of Step 6 is to help you to take a fresh look at your relationships. It looks at the benefits of associating with people who enhance your confidence and will encourage you to add friends to your circle who are supportive and have a positive effect on you. It also looks at ways in which you can improve your relationships with people who are currently in your life but who are less supportive than you would like them to be.

■ Beware of the 'energy vampires'

Your confidence is directly affected by the company you keep. The people in your life influence your thoughts, actions and behaviour. Spend time with people who like and value you and you will feel good about yourself. However, through inertia or habit, you may have people around who put you down and belittle your ideas, treat you badly, make you feel as if you're in a competition you always lose, or are disrespectful or uncaring.

The energy from people who are inspiring and upbeat will rub off on you. People who are pessimistic and negative will drag you down.

Certain 'friends' (otherwise known as 'energy vampires') are people who have somehow become attached to your life, whom you probably would not choose if you were to meet them afresh again. After spending time with them you feel drained and discontented. They are often people who complain a great deal, who use you and don't give anything positive back, or who make themselves feel good at your expense. These people are usually more demanding of your time than your truly good friends, whose company, in contrast, recharges you and makes you feel good about yourself and about life.

Alice – Making time for those who matter most

Alice was so busy that she didn't have a single moment to call her own. It turned out that far too much of her time was devoted to people who fed off her good nature, and demanded a great deal of her attention to sort out their problems, either through hours of advice-giving on the phone or with practical help. Her true friends, knowing how overworked and exhausted she was, had the tact to leave her alone. The result was that she rarely benefited from her life-enhancing relationships because the people she spent her time with held her back.

Because Alice is a kind person she felt an obligation to help anyone who asked, however detrimental this was to herself. It was hard to convince her that for her own sake she needed to be firmer with these people. Her attitude changed, however, when she realized that it meant she had been neglecting the people she cared for most. That horrified her and gave her the strength to stand up to the undue demands that were being placed on her. When the balance changed and she began to see more of the people who made her feel good, and less of the others, the difference in her well-being was evident immediately, even before she had been able to prune her busy schedule.

■ Who do you value in your life?

Like most people, you probably have a mixture of loved ones, friends and colleagues in your life. Some people make you feel good – and some don't. All of them will have had an impact on your life and will continue to have some influence on you. It is helpful to become aware of how people affect you so that you can make informed decisions about who you want to spend time with and see if anything needs to change.

TAKE ACTION: How do people make you feel?

There are probably people in your life who are pleasant enough but who don't give you a buzz, and others who sometimes make you feel bad but not bad enough to make you dread their company. For the moment, concentrate on making two lists, one for those who make you feel really good and the other for those who make you feel really bad.

Who has a positive effect on your life?

Make a list of the people in your life who always make you feel good about yourself. There can be different reasons for this: they might admire and respect you, they might be good fun or gentle and soothing, or they might be people who challenge your thinking and make life seem exciting and full of possibilities. They could be the people you love best and who love you, but not necessarily. An occasional acquaintance or a mentor at work might invariably lift your spirits and make you feel positive about yourself while someone in your family, who is much closer to you, might consistently put you down and make you feel really bad.

Who has a negative effect on your life?

Make a separate list of all the people who consistently leave you feeling insecure, down or used. Occasionally it is hard to see why someone has a negative effect, as they may not be particularly unpleasant. It may be someone whose company you used to enjoy but you feel they have changed, or you have, or circumstances have arisen that now make the relationship unsatisfactory. Trust your instincts here: if contact with them makes you feel bad, then they will drain you. It may be someone you feel stuck with, such as a neighbour, a colleague or a family member, or you may have some choice in the matter which you have not exercised yet.

Choose to know life-enhancing people

Your first list will contain all the people who make you feel good. You must make them your priority. Not only will that be pleasurable for you, these people will boost your confidence. Is it a very short list? If so, this will explain why you are struggling with confidence issues. From now on you need to seek out people who fit this category. The more of these you have in your life, the more your life will change for the better.

■ Creating confident relationships

Be on the lookout for people who have the potential to offer a mutually fulfilling friendship. The aim here is not necessarily to turn them into best friends, but to find room for them in your life as positive contacts and acquaintances. If a closer relationship develops then regard that as a bonus.

There are some people you meet with whom you will feel an instant connection. Some of them will feel it too and will want to be your friend, but others won't. Don't immediately feel that you are to blame if you don't click – there may be a variety of reasons for this that have nothing to do with you. Nevertheless, most people will be flattered and grateful that you've shown you like them.

If your confidence is shaky you will find it hard to initiate such friendships to begin with. Perhaps you have already met a few people who have the right qualities. Are you too shy to develop a relationship with them? Look back at your scores to the confidence quiz that you filled in on page 15 and identify which area of low confidence is making it difficult for you to approach new people. This is one you might like to concentrate on now. Identify the first action you should take to start the process.

Ruth – The email effect

When Ruth decided to extend her circle of life-enhancing friends she began by collecting the business cards of people she felt drawn to. She would send a short, friendly email to them and she was then able to gauge by their response whether a rewarding acquaintanceship was likely to develop.

On page 232 of *Your workbook* there is space for you to ponder on what makes friendships life-enhancing for you.

▨ Creating quality friendships

There are four things you can do straight away to widen your circle of friends and acquaintances.

- Talk to everyone
- Cultivate your neighbours
- Consider new social activities
- Have friendship lunches

Talk to everyone

The people with the widest and most dynamic circle of friends are those who make a habit of talking to almost everyone they come across. Most of the time these encounters are one-offs but the sheer number of people they connect with means that it is inevitable that a few relationships will develop somewhere along the line.

Try a little experiment. Make a pleasant or humorous comment to the person next to you at the bus stop, on the train or at the supermarket. A few people will be grumpy or unresponsive but most will be delighted. If you are naturally shy, this unthreatening action will show you how much people welcome others who take the initiative, and you will see how friendly they can be. You will gain insights into a variety of people and become more relaxed. This practice will help you at social events you find challenging, such as network functions or parties. In itself, peppering your days with nice chats will make you feel the world is a friendlier place and this will reduce your fears and make you more confident.

Aim at first to speak to one stranger every day. You might want to add this to your energy-creating chart. Step it up as you become more relaxed about it, until talking to everyone becomes a natural part of who you are.

Cultivate your neighbours

People can be a source of misery or support. If you make a point of having short, pleasant chats with people who live near you, and those who work in local shops and amenities, they will feel friendly and well motivated towards you. Your quality of life will improve. If a problem develops with someone you will be able to handle it with a reasonable chance of success. If your first contact with them is when you complain about noise or a service, the response is likely to be negative. If people have grown to like you, their reaction will be very different.

Here are a few tips for getting on with your neighbours:

- Learn their names and other key facts about them so that you can enquire after their children, pets or work.
- Ask how they are.
- Let them know a little about yourself ('Work is mad at the moment!') so that they feel there is a real connection.
- Offer help that you can easily give, such as unloading their shopping from the car or watering their plants when they are away. When you have to ask for something in return they'll be pleased to agree.

Consider new social activities

Ask yourself where you are likely to meet the kind of people you'd like to have in your circle. What would their hobbies and interests be? Where would they go for their entertainment? These are the activities and places for you. Once you have identified the best environments to find like-minded people, turn up and try the following:

- Look friendly and approachable.
- Have a normal, human conversation with people – don't try too hard or oversell yourself.
- Respond to other people by showing that you are genuinely listening to them and enjoying their company.
- Don't discriminate and don't make snap judgements. Be open to every-one and avoid assessing people on the way they look, by what they do for a living or in terms of how useful they might be to you.

Make it easier for people to relate to you by disclosing some basic information about yourself. Avoid asking potentially embarrassing personal questions and stick to safe neutral areas, such as the event you are both at, your journey – even the weather – until you know a person better. Sometimes innocent enquiries about someone's marital status, family relationships or employment can offend if they are having problems.

If you hit it off with someone make sure you take a phone number or email address so that you can take the initiative to contact them later.

Have friendship lunches
Set aside a day of the week when you will meet friends for lunch, either those who are already in your circle or the new ones you'd like to know better. Make it a different person each week.

■ How to be a quality friend
To have quality friendships you need to be a life-enhancing person yourself. Here are seven techniques to help you become the sort of friend that other people are looking for:

- Remember your sense of humour
- Be appreciative
- Show an interest
- Always show and expect respect

- Always be honest
- Give your help willingly
- Ask for help

Remember your sense of humour

You don't have to be a joke-factory (which can be off-putting) but people are always attracted to those who are upbeat and ready to laugh. New friendships can be stopped in their tracks if you moan or are overly critical.

Of course, you don't always have to put on a happy face with your long-standing friends, and it can be appropriate to talk to them about your problems or worries, but if this is the tenor of all your conversations you will become an energy vampire yourself. Even good friends might start to dread seeing you until you go back, at least sometimes, to being the cheerful person they first met.

Be appreciative

Let people know what you appreciate about them. Express affection, pay compliments, show admiration, thank them and tell them why something they have said or done has made a difference to you. Some people worry that this might seem creepy or sycophantic, but that will only be the case if you are insincere. If you truly think it, say it. Everyone loves a generous comment and will like you all the more for it.

Where appropriate, send an email or card to express your feelings in writing. You will be pleasantly surprised by the feedback. Accept all compliments that come your way with good grace.

Show an interest

Ask people about themselves and truly listen to what they tell you. Comment on what they've said so they know you've been paying attention and that your interest is genuine. Remember what they tell you so that you can say, 'Whatever happened about . . . ?'

Always show and expect respect

The most enduring relationships are built on genuine mutual respect. This is when you not only like the person but also admire their values, behaviour and ideas. If you don't feel this, then the person can never be a true friend. If people don't respect you they will never be on your life-enhancing list, unless they have other qualities that make them enjoyable on occasions.

Treat everyone with respect anyway. Even if they don't arouse feelings of respect in you, behave as if they do. Listen carefully and don't criticize, put them down, laugh at them, patronize them or show you feel superior. Don't talk about them badly behind their backs. This makes you more respectworthy and trustworthy, and it will be noticed. You will be treated better by most people, including the ones you truly respect.

Always be honest

Don't lie about your qualifications, don't exaggerate your successes and don't express an opinion unless you genuinely believe it. These things may not be important for a casual encounter but misrepresenting yourself is no foundation for real friendship.

Give your help willingly

Look for opportunities to help other people. This doesn't have to involve putting yourself out inordinately. In fact, it's better if it doesn't because if something turns into a duty or a chore you'll only end up feeling resentful. Goodwill is built up when you do something for someone else freely, because it is little trouble to you, not when you are looking for the payback of an immediate favour in return.

Here are a few ideas.

- Make them a drink when you are making one for yourself.
- Lend a book or CD they've shown interest in.
- Give information they need.
- Introduce someone to someone else who can be helpful.
- Offer a tip from your area of expertise.
- Offer to do something you find easy that the other person finds hard, for instance, making a phone call, deciphering a contract, changing a plug.
- Give your time and attention, maybe to offer your opinion on a proposal, to check through a letter they've written, or to help them choose an outfit for a special occasion.

● Send a card of encouragement to arrive on the day of a stressful event or make a quick phone call of support.

Ask for help

People feel warmly towards those they've helped. They feel good about the fact that they have done something positive, or displayed their greater knowledge or experience. And they will like you all the more for making them feel needed and useful. The key is to ask people only for the kind of help that they are likely to provide easily and willingly. It's important not to overstep the mark and exploit their good nature.

■ Dealing with people who drain you

Like Alice (page 120), who neglected her real friends because other people demanded so much of her time and attention, you need to reassess your attitude towards the people on the list of those who drain you. If you don't need to have contact with them, don't. This doesn't necessarily mean being harsh. But once you are aware of the effect they have on you it will be natural for you to reduce the time you spend with them. Cut down on the length of phone calls by saying at the outset that you only have a couple of minutes to spare – and stick to it.

Practise your strategies for setting boundaries and saying no from Step 4: *Be true to yourself*. You need to avoid making promises that you will later regret. If people react badly you may just have to be tough and decide to end the relationship.

There are some people who are firmly in your life, of course, such as family, neighbours or colleagues, and if these are on your list then the challenge is to transform the relationship so that they don't drain you so much.

■ Setting boundaries for energy vampires

There are three main types of energy vampire – the moaners, the crushers and the critics – and we need to be able to stop them making us feel bad.

Managing moaners

If someone is hard to be around because they are always moaning about life, you will give them a chance to change if you point it out. You could say something like, 'When you tell me about all the things you hate or that have gone wrong I feel depressed, too. I'd like us to talk about some positive things.'

If they look blank, pick on something you know is good: 'Tell me about your new kitchen/son's exam results/weekend in the country/the great new hairdresser you've discovered.' Continue to steer them back to the positive whenever they start to moan.

Coping with crushers

Some people love to put you and your ideas down. They say you'll never be able to do what you want, you're aiming too high, that life isn't like that, and so on. They will claim to have your best interests at heart.

Say: 'You may be trying to be helpful but when you tell me that something is impossible I feel bad. What I need to do is make up my own mind about it. I'd really like you just to listen to what I have to say for a while without making any comment. That would be really useful.'

Countering your critics

Family members, colleagues and bosses may criticize you habitually. This, of course, has the effect of making you feel not only miserable and unconfident but, usually, also makes you truculent and unwilling to change to suit them.

With family members or friends, you can say: 'When you criticize me like that I feel attacked and defensive. If something I do bothers you, tell me what it is without attacking my personality or intelligence. If you come up with a suggestion that will make a difference I will be able to consider it.' You may have to repeat this message a number of times before they stop getting at you.

Criticism at work can be even more delicate. One way to deal with it is to say something like: 'If you tell me two things I've done right before you criticize you'll get the best from me as I'll be inspired to work even harder.' The key to asking for a change of attitude is to present it to your boss as a benefit and opportunity, giving it a spin that suggests that it will make you even more efficient in future. In coaching we call this 'managing up' – telling your boss, without whining or complaining, how to get the best out of you. Most people know what they don't like, but they are not so clear about how to raise the subject without creating bad feeling. Think about the solution you want and then take the time to work out how to best present it to your boss.

■ Check your own attitude

Before you set about changing the people in your life, consider what you can do yourself to make things better. After all, this is ultimately the only area where you have any control. You can make requests of other people as clearly and helpfully as you like but after that it's up to them. And there are two key questions you can ask yourself.

Are you an energy vampire?

Look back at the things that drain you about other people. Are you guilty of any of them yourself? Ask yourself: 'Am I an energy vampire?' Make a conscious effort to be a more life-enhancing, quality friend by following the suggestions earlier in this chapter.

Even if you're sure you are not generally a drain on other people, you might find that in the company of energy vampires you become like them. This is natural. We are influenced by the company we keep. We moan with the moaners, we say crushing things in return to the crushers and we offer highly personal criticisms of the people who criticize us. Remember that it's a two-way process: you can influence them, just as they influence you. Treating them as you would wish to be treated yourself can turn out to be more effective than asking them to change. It would certainly be a more subtle approach.

Have you any reason to feel guilty?

Just as it is human nature to warm to someone you have helped or done something nice for, so is the reverse true – quite unfairly you can feel resentment towards people you have treated badly or hurt in some way. This is because guilt makes you feel bad and you don't like them for reminding you of the feeling, even if they say nothing about it. You fear seeing these people, so they become energy drains. In reality, however, it's your problem rather than theirs. Ask yourself: 'Have I any reason to feel guilty?' This is worth tackling even if the incident happened a long time ago. The following techniques should help.

- Acknowledge the wrong, mistake or bad behaviour to yourself.
- Admit it to someone else; this can help you put it in perspective and cement your determination to take responsibility for it.

- Tell the person you've wronged that you are sorry.
- Ask the person what you can do to make amends.

If you can't face a confrontation with the person you've wronged, you could write them a letter instead. Responses may range from surprise on their part (they've virtually forgotten the incident or they didn't mind) to an angry rejection – and anything in between. Whatever the reaction, you will feel better for your action. The act of apologizing and offering to make amends will help to heal your guilty feelings. Having the subject out in the open will usually stop you dreading seeing the other person.

Whether the other person responds well to your apology or not, you can now move on. Feeling guilt after you've done your best to clear things up serves no more purpose and, indeed, can become a habit, just as overworry does. You know it is time to stop feeling guilty when you ask yourself, 'Is there anything more I can do to make amends?' If the answer is yes, then do it. When the answer is truly no, any more obsessing about it is pointless. You can't change what you did or said in the past. You can only affect what happens in the future. You will find, when it takes up no more of your thinking time, that you have removed a large energy drain.

If the person is dead, or you are unable to make contact, then writing the letter is still a powerful way to help you move on. One of my clients wrote a letter to a child she had bullied at school. She had carried the guilt of this for many years. Pouring our her feelings and her shame into a letter made all the difference. Although she still felt bad about what had happened, she was no longer haunted by the memory of the events.

Once you have experienced the relief of doing this, you might want to do the same for other incidents in the past or people no longer in your life. Any memory that causes you guilt and shame is energy-draining. It is powerfully liberating to apologize for your mistakes and make your peace.

Practising confident actions will attract positive reactions.

Step 7
Act confident until you feel confident

❏ The actions that will transform your confidence

❏ Use positive word power

❏ Discover the power of body language

❏ The importance of confident role models

'Suit the action to the word, the word to the action . . . '

William Shakespeare, Hamlet

To believe that you should wait to feel confident before attempting something that makes you nervous, is understandable – but not always necessary. As you know, one of the main messages of this book is that action breeds confidence. This step takes that message further: if you act as if you are confident, even if you don't feel it at the outset, something changes. You will feel your confidence rising and notice that people are reacting to you differently.

Alistair – New thoughts lead to new reactions

Alistair's confidence see-sawed. He knew he was talented and highly intelligent, with excellent qualities, yet he often doubted himself, especially as he wasn't materially successful. He felt at his worst in company, particularly among other people from his profession who were more established then he was. He felt apologetic, defensive, 'less than', a bit of a failure. Sometimes this meant that he didn't know what to say for himself, and he kicked himself afterwards for seeming dull and slow.

At other times Alistair's lack of confidence manifested itself as bravado: he would talk too much or inappropriately or find himself bragging about how well he was doing. He was so self-conscious about his lack of success when he was with other people that he found it impossible to act naturally. He was always waiting for them to put him down.

We discussed how he would behave differently if he was truly confident – if he was successful, well paid and respected in his line of work. At first he said that he thought he would probably be unbearably arrogant. I questioned that. We talked about truly successful people who were approachable, modest and generous to others. Alistair could think of a few people who fitted the bill. He wanted to be that kind of person, someone whose success was obvious and acknowledged by everyone, and someone who was also valued for his kindness and human qualities.

I set Alistair the task of catching the eye of anyone he passed in the street and announcing, silently, that he was like this. The formula he devised was:

'I am respected and successful – and a very nice person!' Fortunately, he was open-minded enough to be prepared to give this a try, although he thought the idea was slightly insane.

Alistair reported back with surprise and pleasure that he had found this a very positive experience. He hadn't consciously done anything different, apart from repeating this phrase in his head as he passed strangers, but he had felt very good and he had also had a sense that in that split-second contact there was a subtle difference in the way people looked at him. He was willing to try the technique again at a forthcoming important social event that was going to be full of bigwigs from his profession.

On the way to the event Alistair practised by repeating the phrase in his head as he looked strangers in the eye, and by the time he arrived he was feeling much more confident. 'It was so strange,' he told me afterwards. 'I noticed people giving me an assessing "Who's that?" look. I was sought out by people I knew and those that I didn't. I was being treated with interest and respect. I stopped thinking the phrase pretty soon – I was too busy. I was able to have relaxed, good conversations. I didn't have to pretend to be anything I wasn't because I felt OK being who I am. I came home thinking, "I really handled that well!"'

What happened? I don't know (and Alistair didn't either) what outward difference there was in the way he presented himself. I can guess, though, that both the expression on his face and his posture were open, welcoming and assured, rather than fearful and apologetic. I suppose that when people talked to him he assumed an attitude that suggested he was glad to talk to them rather than needy. Certainly there was no room in his mind for paralyzing wonderings about whether they thought he was an idiot or a failure – it was full of the thought that he was successful and nice.

While he was feeling like this he didn't have to find words to convince people: they would sense it. We send out wordless messages about ourselves all the time, and other people pick these up instantly at a level they don't even comprehend.

Of course, this didn't transform Alistair's confidence overnight. But he had a technique at his disposal that he could use at any time. He also experienced what confidence felt like and knew that it was within his grasp. As the old saying goes, 'If you always do what you've always done, you'll always get what you always got!' By changing his thoughts and actions, Alistair had proved to himself that he could get different results.

■ Discovering word power

The words we use to, and about, ourselves have a huge emotional impact. Alistair's story illustrates the effect they can have on your confidence and the way you present yourself. When he was designating himself a 'failure' or 'less than' he came across badly and his confidence plummeted. When he chose his magic phrase, 'I am respected and successful – and a very nice person!' the outcome was that he felt better about himself and came across as more confident. The power of words alone is demonstrated by the fact that saying them without even truly believing them was transformational for him.

TAKE ACTION: Confident wordplay: What works for you?

What are the words that best sum up how you feel or want to be described when you are fully confident? Play around with some ideas until you come up with ones that give you a feeling of excitement and put a smile on your face. Work with these words until you have a phrase that sums up the confident you as pithily as possible.

Write it down here if you like.

Keep your phrase to no more than ten words, then try the following two exercises.

Act confident until you feel confident

Think yourself confident – with a silent power phrase

Copy Alistair (page 134) and repeat your preferred phrase in your head as you catch the eye of people you pass in the street. At that moment, be the person you want to be. See how it makes you feel. What is different?

Dee – Silently confident at 40-something

Dee was coming up to her 45th birthday and was feeling unattractive and a little bit past it.

'I've become invisible,' she told me. 'Men's eyes slide past me in the street.' The phrase she chose was the aspirational, 'I'm a gorgeous woman in my sexual prime!' She could feel the difference in herself as she said it silently. 'I felt my body straighten, I walked with more pride,' she said. 'It tickled me and I think I must have had a little smile on my face. I wasn't anxiously searching men's faces to see whether they were noticing me. I felt powerful, I was telling them who I was. I didn't mind when people didn't return my look. In those moments I felt it was their loss not noticing this gorgeous woman. But in fact many more people did return my glance in a way that made me feel good.'

Write down your power phrase

You might want to put your phrase in your diary or on a card. Look at it when you want to revive your confidence. If it's short and pithy it will be easy to remember and you can repeat it like a mantra when you want to remind yourself where you are heading.

Fran – The best in the business

Fran's mantra was 'The best editor in the business!' Whenever she repeated this to herself she found it affected the journalistic decisions she made and the actions she took. Her image of how the best magazine editor would behave in any given situation brought out the best in her.

You can devise some powerful phrases for yourself in *The confident you* on page 233 of *Your workbook*.

■ Learn to use body language

Just as choosing powerful words has an effect on the way you project yourself, so changing the way you move affects your feelings and thoughts.

Body language is the way we communicate with each other, usually unconsciously, without words. The way you move, gesture and stand tells the world what you think of yourself – and how you are reacting to other people. Interpreting body language has become a science only relatively recently but everyone is a natural expert in it, even those who've never heard the term. You will pick up signals from other people faster than you are aware. All you may be aware of is that you are drawn to someone – feel happy and comfortable in their company – or are strangely put off, while all the time you are giving out signals of your own. Research shows that as much as 65 per cent of face-to-face conversation may be conveyed by facial expressions and other elements of body language.

If you feel bad about yourself it shows in your body language. When you are unconfident you carry yourself differently. In an attempt to look smaller, or not draw attention to yourself, you slump or keep your head lowered. When you enter a room you may scuttle, or slink in cautiously, and then place yourself in a corner or immediately find a seat. Your silent message is: 'Keep away!'

And what happens when you find yourself talking to someone? If your eyes slide away from contact, you stand with your arms crossed over your chest or you clutch a bag, glass or plate tightly to you, your body language is explaining that you feel defensive, uncomfortable, closed to communication. 'Reading' this makes the other person uncomfortable too and so they'll soon be off. Or you may fix them with a desperate gaze and lean forward too eagerly in an attempt to keep them with you. Your body language screams neediness and this will make people look for ways to escape the trap.

Lynn – Transforming angry body language

Lynn discovered the truth of this for herself. After the failure of her marriage she put on a lot of weight. 'I was upset because I felt unfeminine, and that made me angry,' she said. 'I didn't even have to know a guy to think, "You're so superficial – you won't even give me a second glance now but you would have been all over me when I was thinner!"'

Men did indeed give her a wide berth but she had misinterpreted the signals. It had nothing to do with her excess weight but everything to do with her extremely hostile body language. Lynn held her head so high that her chin jutted forward. She looked at men challengingly and unsmilingly, often with one hand on her hip, and she swayed away from them as they talked, almost as if they had bad breath.

When she watched herself on the video of a friend's wedding she got a shock. 'It was months later. I'd lost some weight and was feeling better about myself,' she said. 'I had a new boyfriend and he was watching with me. He said, "Wow: what was the matter with you?" I said, "Oh, I was much fatter then." He said, "Really, were you? But I mean you look so cross! What were you so annoyed about?" He barely noticed the extra weight but he did say he wouldn't have dared approach me then. And I could see why: even I wouldn't have wanted to talk to me!'

The interesting thing is that changing your body language not only gives more positive signals – it can also change the way you feel and think.

In an experiment, a group of students were asked to listen to the same lecture. Half were asked to sit with their arms folded across their chests (a negative, closed posture), while the other half were encouraged to be relaxed, with their arms and legs uncrossed. It was shown that the group with the negative posture learned significantly less than the relaxed group and were far more critical of the lecturer. Their way of sitting had created a closed, hostile state of mind. The more relaxed group got a great deal more out of the lecture.

TAKE ACTION: Practise positive posture

You can try this experiment for yourself. Sit down and slump. Hang your head and look at the floor. Now tell yourself you're happy. Doesn't it feel odd?

Now change your position. Sit erect with a smile on your face. Look up to the ceiling. While you are holding this pose try to make yourself feel depressed. Doesn't this seem even odder, almost ludicrous?

■ Developing confident posture

You are likely to be most aware of your posture when out in public, at a meeting or a party, when you want to come across as attractively confident.

We've all known people who seem to be incredibly attractive to others despite not being conventionally good-looking and well turned out. What all of them have in common, however, is that they think they are attractive. It's not a question of drawing other people into their own fantasies but a demonstration of the simple fact that feeling confident and looking at ease in your own body is attractive in itself: someone who feels attractive *is* attractive.

The scene is a party. There are two women, so similar they could be sisters – roughly the same age, about the same weight (rather heavier than the ideal) – wearing almost identical black dresses. They are both fairly pretty but one of the women always seems to have two or three men in attendance while the other one scarcely attracts a second glance and only talks to the couple of people she already knows. What's the secret?

We've all been perplexed at times by the seemingly inexplicable success of a perfectly ordinary woman. Is it her cleavage? Is she an outrageous flirt? The reason, nine times out of ten, is more subtle – it's her body language. At that party the second woman was feeling defeated before she arrived. She had recently put on weight, and she felt apologetic and unattractive. Her body language screamed: 'Don't look at me!' so people didn't. By contrast, the first woman was excited and felt confident. She was probably unaware of how these positive feelings affected every move she made but the result was that she became a magnet for the men.

Men are no different to women when it comes to body language. Two men can be similar in height, age, weight and good looks (or lack of them) yet people drift away from one of them after a short conversation while the other is constantly surrounded.

So how can you act as if you are the person who is quietly confident in their own powers of attraction and approachability? You can start by looking at yourself long and hard in the mirror (or, like Lynn on page 138, on video). What is your posture saying? Begin retraining yourself to sit and stand properly. Be aware of how you walk. Then watch and learn from attractively confident people. Copy what they do and you'll not only give out more positive signals, you'll begin to feel better about yourself. The truly empowered person exudes poise that is apparent to others. These are the things you'll notice when you look at people with positive body language:

- They make an entrance by walking into a room confidently.
- They smile, look pleased to be there, and survey the room and the people in it with interest.
- They position themselves where others can see them rather than hiding away.
- They stay physically relaxed and loose rather than rigid, whether they are standing, moving or sitting.
- They don't fidget but maintain a confident posture, which makes them appear non-aggressive and welcoming.
- They introduce themselves to others first rather than waiting for people to approach them.
- They make frequent eye contact with everyone they speak to and leave their hands free to gesture.
- They make encouraging hand movements that are open, with the wrists and palms facing upwards rather than balled into fists.
- They occasionally touch the person they are speaking to gently on the arm.
- They lean slightly towards the person they are talking to, especially when both are sitting down.
- They don't sit with their arms or legs crossed, or if they do cross their legs, they incline them towards the other person.

It's tempting to arm yourself with a glass of wine or a plate of food at a party as it gives you something to do, but, as Leil Lowndes points out in her book *How to Talk to Anyone*, animals give each other a wide berth when one of them is eating, and humans have the same instinct. Similarly, if you are insecure and shy you might prefer to cope by taking a plate of food round. But while you will say, 'Would you like a canapé?' to dozens of strangers, the contact is unlikely to be very meaningful. Your body language is saying 'I'm busy' and most people will leave you to it.

So what should you do? The first thing to do is to smile. It's been proven that the action of smiling, even if it's not genuine at the beginning, actually lifts your mood and gives the strongest body language message. Your smile says: 'I like being me – and I like you.'

Michael Neill suggests paying a silent compliment to people. As with having a phrase about yourself in your mind, thinking something nice about someone else also affects the expression on your face and subtly alters your attitude. Admittedly, finding something nice might sometimes be a challenge but that's part of the fun. Perhaps it's something they are wearing, or they look awkward and you can acknowledge their courage for attending, or they have an infectious laugh that's appealing.

I love this tip: by searching for something good to think about people I find I naturally feel warmer towards them. Have a look at the people who are clearly doing the opposite (much more common) – that look of contempt, cool assessment and lack of interest makes them less attractive. It's not necessary to say the compliment out loud – you will feel the effect by merely thinking it.

▦ Listen to your body – and relax

Tension in the body transmits tense signals to the brain making you feel even more worried and unconfident. Spotting when and where you've tensed up and then consciously relaxing your muscles will give you an instant feeling of well-being, and the change in your body language will make people react to you differently.

Exercise, particularly a stretching programme such as Pilates or the Alexander technique, will affect your posture for the better. Pilates will make you aware of your muscles and how you use them. The Alexander technique is a gentle retraining of the way you use your body. One of its main aims is to banish tension along with improving your posture. As a bonus, as your muscles are coaxed to lengthen you can find yourself anything up to an inch taller.

Breathe differently. Confident, happy breathing is deep and slow. Place your hand on your abdomen and feel it expand as you breathe in. You'll stop feeling anxious. Yoga offers techniques for improving breathing and is worth looking at.

The more you practise changing your posture to a more confident, relaxed stance, the more natural it will become. Remind yourself to do this when you are alone, while you're cooking, for example, or washing up or cleaning your teeth. Remember to check yourself frequently as you go about your daily business. Glance at your reflection in shop windows and straighten up if you notice your posture has slipped. Confident posture should not just be for special occasions.

■ Choose a confident role model

Who do you admire? Who embodies how you'd like to be when you are confident? It could be a famous person (alive or dead), someone you know or even a character from a film or novel. In a given situation, how would your role model behave? What would they say? Acting as if you are your role model can be a potent way to try out new behaviour. What it also does is take your attention away from yourself and your feelings of insecurity as your brain searches for the different action and behaviour. It makes you more objective, less self-conscious and therefore – paradoxically – more natural.

You might find one person who embodies everything you want to be or you may opt for a series of people, each one relevant to a different area of your life.

Linda – Three role models for three stages of life

Linda had three role models. The first one was an ex-boss who had created a wonderful, stimulating atmosphere that brought out the best in people. In her professional life Linda often asked herself what this man would have done or said, and was able to put herself in his shoes. Then there was an actress whom Linda admired for her looks and vivacity, and the apparent ease with which she handled growing older. Evoking this woman's image was particularly powerful for Linda when she made decisions about her diet, activity levels and the way she presented herself. When she'd given herself goals for losing weight and taking more exercise, they'd seemed daunting and uninspiring but when she thought of herself as the actress the choices became easier. She also took more care of her general appearance. Would the actress have postponed doing anything about looking good until she was the perfect shape? Of course not! Linda's mother had been a wonderful example of motherhood but she had never worked outside the home, so Linda's third role model was someone she knew who had successfully combined family and a career.

TAKE ACTION: Three steps to finding your ideal role model

1 Make a list of people you admire

Take some time to think about the people you could use as role models. Imagine yourself in many different situations and choose someone for each area of your life. Write the names down. This will lock them into your consciousness so that you can bring up their image whenever you want to.

2 Step into their shoes

Choose one of the people on your role-model list. Imagine that they are standing in front of you. Step forward into that space – and into their shoes. You are now your role model. Look around and ask yourself:

How do you see your world?
What thoughts run through your mind?
What do you believe about yourself and about life?
How do you feel?
How are you standing?
What might you say?

Fully experience the difference. If you've never done anything like this before you will be surprised to discover that you don't need any acting talent. This simple action transports you into another way of thinking and being, releasing you to 'know' things that don't otherwise occur to you. Once you've experienced the power of this you know that you can choose to act as if you are this person, at any time that serves you.

3 Practise in real situations

When a testing occasion is coming up, prepare for it by stepping into your role model's shoes.

● As you arrive at the party 'become' the person you admire, who is easy and confident.

● Before the job interview start to act as if you are the relaxed and secure role model they'd love to have in the job.

● When you are about to set a boundary, evoke the feelings and behaviour of the person you've identified who is reasonable and sympathetic yet firm.

The role model who inspires you needs to be appropriate only to you. Barry, a systems analyst, chose to act as if he were Frank Sinatra when he went for interviews. This didn't mean he had to burst into song! For him Sinatra personified effortless, masculine confidence, and warmth, humour, talent and dedication.

TAKE ACTION: Become your own role model

It can be just as effective to be your own role model, using what you already know about confidence. When you look back at your scores in the confidence quiz on page 15 you will probably find an area or two where your confidence is reasonably high. If not, you can probably go back to a time you remember when it was. How are you, or were you, different in those areas? What can you learn from yourself that you can use in the situations where your confidence fails you? Knowing that you can take lessons from yourself is very empowering.

Here are three techniques to help you to be your own role model.

1 Anchor yourself in confident mode

Choose a situation where you are usually confident or remind yourself of a specific situation where you were able to demonstrate this. Step into that moment and relive it, and ask yourself:

What did you see?
What did you hear?
What reactions did you elicit from the other people present?
How are you feeling now as you imagine it?

For instance, you might think back to a time with close friends when communication is effortless and pleasant. You are interesting and charming, engaged and warm. Everyone is feeling good, especially you. You see smiling faces around you, the conversation is easy and relaxed; everyone has their turn. You are not worrying about what you say but you have trust in yourself. You accept and like the people around you, and feel that they accept and like you, too.

In a practice known as neurolinguistic programming (or by its initials, NLP) it is suggested that you 'anchor' this feeling. When you are fully in the experience, clench your fist or make an 'O' with your thumb and forefinger, and associate the sensations with how you are feeling. When you want to re-experience the feeling, 'fire' the 'anchor' by repeating the gesture. When you practise this it becomes a short cut to those good feelings.

2 Transform a past experience

Pick another situation where you wished you'd been more confident but weren't. For instance, you might imagine yourself at the last work meeting you attended, when you feel you failed yourself in some way. What would happen if you could superimpose that relaxed, happy and confident mood with your friends on to that occasion? Step back and ask yourself:

How would you feel in that situation now?
What would you do, say or think differently?
How would you hold yourself?
How would you breathe?
What sort of expression would be on your face?
How would you be less fearful and more brave?

3 Practise changing your attitude

Use what you have learnt about how you can transfer confidence from one situation on to another. Before a stressful situation take yourself back to a happy and confident time, and put yourself into the state of mind you had then.

One thing you experience in these exercises is that confidence is an attitude. Change your attitude and your behaviour and your demeanour become confident, too.

Emily used the anchoring technique in social situations where she felt so unconfident that she was likely to drink too much and be tempted to smoke (she was giving up). Her 'anchor' was a pretty little bracelet she'd bought for the purpose. When she touched or twisted it on her wrist she would be reminded of her confident state. She noticed especially that her breathing would immediately slow down and her shoulders would relax.

■ Dress to look your best

How you present yourself affects your confidence and affects how other people perceive you. Only someone who is supremely confident can get away with looking bedraggled and uncared for. Even then, they might be dismissed or undervalued. Most of us, however, want to look our best.

It's a boost when you feel you're looking good. When you are well groomed and dressed in shapes and colours that flatter you, you are already halfway to feeling confident. On the other hand, if you feel you're looking scruffy and ill-kempt, you're unlikely to feel good about yourself or elicit respectful attention.

It shouldn't matter, but it does. For instance, career coaches recommend that you dress appropriately for the post you aspire to, not the one you're in. The receptionist who dresses like a manager is more likely to be taken seriously and rise through the ranks faster.

Good grooming doesn't have to be costly. Here are seven useful tips to help you look your best on a budget, whatever the occasion.

- Pay attention to your hair, skin and teeth so that you always look healthy and attractive.
- Make sure you are always clean and pleasant-smelling. Women in particular get a boost if their skin feels good – use creams and lotions to make it silky smooth and a pleasure to touch, and a loofah to improve its texture.

- Check that everything you wear is in good repair: shoes polished and heeled, missing or loose buttons attended to, clothes freshly washed and pressed or dry-cleaned. Carry out a maintenance inspection of your wardrobe regularly so that you can always look presentable at short notice.
- Dress appropriately: formal for formal, businesslike for professional and the right degree of casual for dressing-down occasions.
- Choose colours that flatter you. If you need help with this ask a friend, use an in-store shopping adviser or treat yourself to a consultation with a professional colour expert.
- Be guided by what suits you rather than what is in fashion – unless fashion is your business. Conventional shapes that flatter you will do more for your image than the latest, must-have designer garment.
- Be comfortable. Avoid clothes that are too tight and shoes that hurt your feet, or outfits you feel too hot or too chilly in. They might give you a lift when you look in the mirror but any discomfort will show in your face and your posture. You should aim to feel so at ease with the look and feel of what you are wearing that you can completely forget about it.

If you consistently act 'as if' by changing your thoughts, words, body language and what you wear, you will create new habits of being. Eventually, this will cease to be acting. It will become real: part of you.

Start where you are:
if you enjoy and
appreciate life as it is today,
you will become happier
and more confident.

Step 8
Live confidently now

❏ What do we mean by success?
❏ How to be happy
❏ Accepting yourself and letting go

'In our daily lives, we must see that it is not happiness that makes us grateful, but the gratefulness that makes us happy.'

Albert Clarke

My first ambition was to be a child prodigy, a measurement of success that is ruthlessly inflexible in terms of deadline. I knew it was all over by the age of 14 when I wasn't making headlines nor anyone gasp, except about the state of my bedroom and my capacity to sleep round the clock on weekends.

■ What do we mean by success?

The issue of what success and happiness are has always interested me. For years I had ideas about when these desirable attributes would be mine. They always involved things I would achieve or have in my life. It so happened that I attained many of these desired elements, but usually only after I'd stopped really wanting them fiercely. At first there would be a fleeting, warm glow of achievement, followed by a so-whattish sense that I could cross something off my list, but I was always left with a feeling that real success and happiness were yet to come.

Over the years I've radically revised my definition of success, especially since I started working as a coach helping other people on their own paths.

Catherine – A matter of priority

Catherine came to me for coaching because she felt her marriage was in trouble. She had one child and was feeling broody again, and she wanted to fix her relationship with her husband so that he would agree to have another baby. Professionally, she was wildly successful – loads of money and loads of clients, all achieved, it seemed, effortlessly. I was thrilled for her.

I asked Catherine to set aside one hour a week with her husband so that they could start to tackle their problems. She stared at her diary and told me that that would be impossible. She could only commit half an hour a week to talk to me, she said, and during those sessions I would have to come up with solutions to make her marriage work again – and these had to be of the type that would take up no more of her time. Impossible.

In response I suggested that she should apply the professional skills that she manifestly possessed to finding some extra time to sort out her personal life. Catherine was not willing to do this so I was unable to work with her. She knew what she needed for happiness now – a better relationship with her husband – but she was unable to see that she should prioritize it.

Since my early coaching days, one of my definitions of success and happiness has been to put time where it matters most – in the relationships at the heart of your life. This is what Vicky has done.

Vicky – A zest for life

Vicky has none of the outward trappings of success, but she has a remarkable zest for life and the most ordinary aspects of it. I remember her once rhapsodizing about a beautiful puddle she'd seen, streaked with oil, that shimmered with rainbow colours. When she turned her attention away from what she hadn't got – the reason she came for coaching – to the bounty she had already, and her own gift for enjoying life, she became motivated, happy and confident. She set about improving what was bothering her, but without a discontented yearning for some big future change. Her confidence, previously very low, soared so much that her husband (who had thought coaching a waste of money) was delighted that she continued with it. To the outside world there was not a great difference in her life, but her interior world was radically transformed. The definition of success and happiness that I learnt from her is that enjoying and appreciating life as it is today is the pinnacle of achievement.

Success, I believe now, is not about setting a goal and reaching it but about delighting in the journey. It's about being comfortable in your own skin and taking charge of what is getting in the way of you fully appreciating the life you are already living. I believe that whatever happens, even tragedy, can be an opportunity to appreciate more and live more fully. Yet I'm still learning. I still get wound up, anxious and irritable – a small and selfish and unconfident life-state – but whenever I remind myself to go back to basics and take charge of the quality of my daily life everything opens up wonderfully.

> One of my personal icons is my mother, who was savagely attacked by a mugger who shattered her leg when she was 73. She looked back on that incident as a blessing that spurred her to change her life and enjoy the present even more.

I always ask my clients to tell me what is getting in the way of them being happy now. There are the big things: hating the job, wanting to find a partner, real money worries, a major goal that seems unreachable. But so often it's also a mundane collection of daily irritants to do with mess, lack of time, aggravations with family or colleagues, unkept promises to themselves about health and fitness. We work through the exercises outlined in Step 2: *Increase your energy*. However dubious they are at the start, people soon find themselves excited by the improvement in the quality of their daily lives, and the sense of being in control of their own happiness. Tackling the big things then becomes manageable, enjoyable even.

When you decide to make your life a success just as it is, a curious thing happens. The usual success yardsticks not only lose their glamour for you but also paradoxically become easier to attain. I've seen people effortlessly climb higher once they've sorted out their priorities and stopped worrying so much. And, just as inspiring, I've seen people realize they don't want more because they discover they've got all that matters already.

This chapter looks more closely at how you can make your life as good as it can possibly be, just as it is. This is not only a recipe for more happiness and confidence now, but will also affect the bigger changes you want to make in your life for the future.

Tania – Goals can change when you focus on being happy

Tania used to be an academic. She had a job at a university in New York that she wasn't enjoying, and she was struggling to finish her PhD dissertation. What she really wanted was to be an astrologer but she couldn't imagine ever being able to make money at it.

The first thing Tania said to me was: 'I've written 63 pages of my dissertation, but I need to draft 250 in the next three months. It's a drag as I've thought it all through in my mind and feel done with it. I'm seriously procrastinating, planning my wedding, which is in two months, instead of working. I'm full of good intentions and know about time management, but then I fall off and get seriously behind. What do I need – willpower? A magic pill?'

I was struck by the casual way Tania dismissed her wedding preparations as procrastination. 'Suppose you never did finish your dissertation,' I suggested. 'How would that affect your life and your career?'

Tania was shocked. 'I'd never forgive myself,' she said. But she went on to think about it, and had to admit that ultimately it would make very little difference. I invited her to look back at her life from a vantage point of 20 years hence and see which she would consider more important – her dissertation or the wedding. 'Marrying Chris, unquestionably,' she decided.

This acknowledgement of what she really wanted allowed Tania to think the unthinkable: she would spend less time worrying about her dissertation and allow herself more time to work on her wedding plans. Procrastination often happens when you think you should be working on something all day, every day. Tania was prepared to 'put the dissertation in a box' – she would set aside three days a week for this work and try not to get anxious about her lack of progress.

The next week Tania reported that she'd actually done more on her dissertation in the first three days than she had in weeks of believing that she should devote all her time to it, including weekends. Not only that, she'd felt so thrilled and relieved about permitting herself to prepare for her wedding, and daydream about it, that her depression had lifted. 'I've been setting totally unattainable goals every week, thus never getting to feel good about my progress,' she said. 'Worse – I haven't been allowed to feel celebratory about my wedding, just sad that my negative self-image and anxiety is seeping into every area of my life, making me so depressed that I've been afraid Chris will leave me.

He actually said how relieved he was to have my old self back. He thought I was getting cold feet about marrying him!'

I commented that the run-up to a wedding was always stressful, however much two people loved each other, and that misgivings were a natural part of this, which couples rarely discussed. I suggested that she and Chris should set aside one evening a week to talk through any fears that had arisen.

That week Tania also felt able to lift her eyes to the future. She talked about her dream: to make her living working with astrology, which she loved and for which she had real flair. She already had a small and devoted clientele, yet feared that being an astrologer could be unlucrative.

For this reason she believed she needed to commit herself to astrology full-time or not at all – she would have to look for a 'proper' job using her editing or computer skills. Instead, we decided that she would mark one day in her diary as an astrology day, in which she would see clients, prepare for them, work on her astrology website or do more of the academic astrological research that she loved. When the dissertation was finished she would take a part-time job until she developed her astrology practice. 'That feels so much more doable – and fun,' she said. 'It was all getting so heavy in my mind before.'

At the next session Tania was buzzing with the excitement of working on her website and receiving unexpected referrals for astrological readings. But she was starting to worry about her dissertation again. 'Chris's parents came to stay, so I didn't do a thing on it. I really need help to crack it now, once and for all,' she said. 'Working on it just three days a week has helped but last week was a washout and I need to catch up. When I'm working well, I can easily do six to eight pages a day – 24 in a three-day week – and I'm frustrated when I don't.'

I pointed out that this was what had made her feel so bad before: setting unrealistic targets, which she failed to meet: 'Rather than basing your target on peak performance, you need to find your resting rate. Spend a day working on your dissertation in an unrushed way and see how many pages you produce. Base your weekly target on that. If it's only one page, so be it – then three pages is what you can expect to achieve and everything else is a bonus.' Tania thought three pages a week would be grim, but she could see she'd feel good setting a target she could realistically beat.

We also discussed ways she could make it easier for herself to produce more. Having identified that phone calls ate into her time, she decided to take her laptop to the library and work there. Another thing that worried her was how PMS would affect her productivity. She always felt depressed and lethargic for a couple of days when her period was due. I suggested that she should plan for this, scheduling easy and pleasant things to do on those days rather than writing her dissertation.

Tania's tutor normally supervised her work in progress and he always galvanized her by setting deadlines. As he was currently out of the country I asked Tania to think of someone who could perform this deadline-orienting function for her, and she decided to enlist her father. I also recommended one of coach Mark Forster's time-management tips, which is to work in ten-minute bursts, rotating the projects of the day. This makes things seem much less daunting as the tasks are broken down into manageable chunks instead of looming like a solid block of hard slog.

Tania told me that she had heard of two part-time jobs that might suit her while she was building up her astrology practice. I talked her through a radical revision of her over-academic CV to highlight different skills and achievements that would be relevant to her change of career. This was all part of the year-long plan that looked forward to a time when she had finished her dissertation, and could leave her university job and began her new life as a professional astrologer.

On the final call Tania described a breakthrough with her dissertation. 'Testing for my "resting rate" completely changed my attitude to it,' she said. 'Instead of rushing to complete a certain amount of pages, I worked with more care. I thought about each sentence, revised more, took my time – and, you know, for the first time I actually enjoyed the writing of it. I'm excited about what I'm doing again. I've asked for more time to finish it. As you promised, knowing I only had to do ten minutes got me started and broke the block each day. Then I found it wasn't necessary, I was motivated to work continuously.'

Something else had helped as well. When Tania had done the unthinkable, and had applied to extend the deadline for submitting her dissertation, this had changed her attitude to the whole university experience. 'I've had this thing in my head that I have to tie up the PhD and work in the department, which I hate, before my life can begin,' she said. 'I've had this lousy year stretching ahead of me, and that's one of the reasons I've been finding it all such a slog. Now I've given myself permission to postpone finishing my dissertation,

I realize I don't have to do the other things, either. I'm going to apply for those part-time jobs and give my attention to building my astrology practice immediately.'

All this had fully released Tania to enjoy the run-up to her wedding, which was now only four weeks away. *'Chris and I have continued the weekly talks about what's come up for us,'* she said. *'We do it on Fridays over a bottle of wine and it's made us incredibly more relaxed about it all. It's legitimized the fact that from time to time it's natural to have fears and misgivings about marrying, but talking about them blows them away. It's something we definitely want to continue after we're married.'*

Tania and I only worked together for one month, but concentrating on improving her daily life and what was making her feel dissatisfied and unconfident, transformed her. It made it possible for her to go for a goal that had previously seemed distant and unattainable.

■ Do you enjoy the 'here and now'?

If you are discontented with yourself and your life, you will inevitably be spending a lot of time thinking about what is wrong. It is human nature to take for granted whatever is not causing a problem and expend valuable energy planning how to put things that are causing problems right. You will be examining what is bothering you, and how you can handle it, but first it is important to see and value what you have right now.

TAKE ACTION: Recognize and count your blessings

Write down everything and everyone you have in your life right now that is good and positive.

Spend some time making this list a really long one. Include the smallest details – the view from your bathroom window, if you particularly like it. Include also the things you like about yourself – your feet, if they are your hidden pride and joy.

Contemplate your list and realize just how lucky you are right now.

To continue this process start a *Gratitude log* on page 234 of *Your workbook*.

■ Allow yourself to savour life's pleasures

People who are constantly dissatisfied overlook the things they enjoy. What they desire is whatever they do not have right now. Once they acquire something they've desired it no longer seems so desirable.

Similarly, we often deny ourselves the enjoyment of our pleasures. If something is a pleasure to you, savour it. Consider how lucky you are to be able to indulge it. Paradoxically, people who are on a diet often eat more of the forbidden foods than they did previously. Their guilt at breaking the diet destroys their pleasure in eating them, so they wolf even more of them down to try to capture the elusive pleasure. If, instead, they concentrated on enjoying the foods they would derive enough satisfaction to be able to be moderate.

What do you enjoy but perhaps deny yourself, or punish yourself for doing, because it's not work or highbrow? I'm assuming, of course, that it's not illegal, self-destructive or unpleasant to other people! There are many simple, harmless pleasures, such as having a long lazy bath, chatting to a friend on the phone or reading a scandalous tabloid instead of a serious newspaper. Confident people allow themselves these pleasures and indulgences. You will be happier and more confident when you do likewise.

■ What's getting in the way of your happiness right now?

Looking at the areas of your life that are causing you trouble, and seeing whether and how you can fix them, is an essential element in improving what is. The quality of your relationships, on all levels, is a great determinant of your happiness now. Positive love relationships and good interactions with colleagues and friends not only support you but help you feel that life is good.

These are some fresh ways of looking at the issue:

Choose to be what you want others to be

If you look for others to behave in certain ways before you do so yourself you may often be disappointed. If you want someone to be loving to you, allow yourself to be as loving as you can for no reason at all – not for the payback. You will instantly feel happier. React to colleagues in the way you wish them to react to you; if they are rude or unfriendly, don't take your cue from them, set the standard yourself.

As Aboodi Shaby, a coach who specializes in exploring happiness, wrote in his newsletter:

> One of the things people often want to talk with me about is how to deal with someone with whom they are experiencing difficulties. So I often get asked questions like 'How do I deal with my difficult husband?', or 'I don't know how to deal with someone at work who always treats me badly.'
>
> My most likely response to these kinds of questions is to suggest that it's not the difficult other person that we have to deal with – it's ourselves! If there is someone in my life who is causing me difficulty, who is upsetting me in some way, then the person I really have to deal with is me!
>
> Something we have to accept is that we can't change others. Certainly, I cannot change you any more than I can change the weather or the landscape. What I can change is my relationship to the weather, my relationship to the person who is causing me to feel upset.
>
> I suggest that there are a few benefits to this different approach. One is that, by realizing that it's ourselves we have to deal with, we are taking fuller responsibility for ourselves – we are not going to get so caught in the 'It's their fault that I am unhappy' conversation that is the cause of a lot of suffering.
>
> We might even notice that it is us and not them who is at the root of our unhappiness in that situation – or, to be more precise, it's our relationship with the 'difficult' boss, for instance, that is the cause of our suffering. We might also be reminded that our happiness does not lie in having people, or any other elements of the outside world, change in order to suit us. Other people (and the world) are how they are, and it's up to us how we interpret and judge them.

Look for the positive in others

You can often turn a situation around by looking for the positive in the people who are causing you difficulties, just as you did when you looked at what positive things you have going for you in your life now. I say this to clients who are complaining about their partners. I ask them to write a list of anything they do value and admire about the other person. Even the angriest person will find something good to say. And the act of highlighting these good things will make a significant change to how they perceive the relationship. Where appropriate, I suggest they offer their list to their partners.

This is possible with even the most difficult people. I once interviewed Aboodi Shaby for a column on coaching I was writing for *The Times*. He gave me a good example of the way in which searching for the positive can transform a negative relationship.

Jeremy – Praise, don't criticize

Jeremy, a client of Aboodi's, came to him with a problem over his boss. 'He's such a jerk,' Jeremy said. 'He's a control freak. He watches over me constantly – I have no time or space to get on in my own way with my work, which, incidentally, I'm excellent at. He always wants to know what I'm doing. And he's so grudging. It would kill him to say "You're doing a great job, Jeremy!" I feel angry, and stuck, and I don't know what to do with these feelings.'

Jeremy's most pressing concern was the impotent anger he felt at the way his boss was treating him. Aboodi's opinion was that Jeremy's hostile feelings towards his boss and his habitual complaining were actually harming him and keeping him stuck. 'Tell me something you admire about your boss – something he does well,' he said. Jeremy was taken aback. 'The man's an asshole,' he insisted. 'What can I say?'

Aboodi pressed him further. After much thought, Jeremy was prepared to acknowledge that his boss did have some things going for him. 'He's extremely logical,' he conceded. 'He's incredibly good on detail. He's articulate.'

Aboodi explained: 'One of the things you can do is build on the future – that's about looking for other work – but let's see what you can do now to make the present perfect. You've got this boss, he's a jerk, but the question is: what can you do to change that?' He suggested Jeremy should look for an opportunity to tell his boss that he'd noticed the strengths he'd identified. 'He will have sensed your hostility, even though you've said nothing,' said Aboodi. 'You're getting no acknowledgement of your worth from him, but he needs acknowledgement too. You can change the negative dynamic by being the one to start the process.' The important point was for Jeremy to choose something he genuinely admired rather than be insincere. He was prepared to give it a go.

The next week he reported that he'd found a moment when it had seemed natural to comment on his boss's abilities. *'We were going through a directive that came from on high, and he spotted some errors and things that needed clarifying before we could implement it,'* he explained. *'You know, I really felt something shift when I told him how good he was at that kind of logical, detailed work. He was obviously pleased. Things have felt a whole lot easier since then. I'm delighted by the impact it had. He's certainly not on my back in the same way.'*

That this had made a real difference was confirmed the following week. Jeremy's boss had been taking the time to chat to him more and one day he said that there was an opening at their Tokyo office. *'He said he thought I was the right man for the job,'* said Jeremy, *'and wanted to know whether I was interested, so that he could put in a good word for me!'*

Let people know what you admire about them

Find an opportunity to tell the difficult people in your life anything that you genuinely appreciate about them. Don't make it up. Be sure it's true. Notice the difference this makes.

■ Change things for the better at work

If you have to work you will want it to be interesting, challenging and fulfilling. You want to make a good living, of course, but you also want to enjoy what you do. When work is really getting you down it often seems as if your only option is to leave. Sometimes that is the right thing to do, as Tania (page 155) discovered, but you can rarely do so instantly. You have to work out your notice. I always encourage my clients to turn the situation around before they leave. If you can leave having changed things for the better your confidence will rise, and you will be able to move forward into your new life much more easily.

I frequently find that when people make these changes they may revise their plans to leave. After making things better at work they decide they are content there after all.

Set your own high standards

This might be the last thing you feel like when your boss or colleagues are unpleasant, but you will strengthen your hand by doing the best possible job, whether you want to leave or simply change things for the better.

There's a temptation to show your dissatisfaction at work by becoming the worker from hell. The problem is that long 'protest' lunches, coming in late, flouting rules, working to rule, being disagreeable, and so on, will simply label you as inefficient. It will mean you won't be listened to when you ask for changes. It will also erode your own confidence. If you're not doing a good job you will become far more nervous about your abilities when it comes to applying for one elsewhere.

It's much better to do your best, despite the circumstances. Set your own standards and live up to them. How do you want to be treated? Treat others like that. Enhance your reputation and support by collaborating with colleagues rather than competing with them. Colleagues will support you, and your boss will be more inclined to listen, if you set a good example. And just in case your boss is oblivious, start to document your accomplishments – don't assume people know about them. Regularly present what you've achieved in a memo, with indisputable, measurable facts. This will also serve as a handy reference when you go for another job.

Improving self-employment

If you are self-employed, behave like an exceptional boss. What if you were employing someone else to do what you do? How would you attract a good candidate and make sure they were happy at their work? Have some fun with this. Draw up excellent conditions of employment and a reward package. See how this affects the quality of your work.

■ Problems with yourself – health, well-being and home

You will have documented your dissatisfactions in core low confidence areas when you were working through Step 2: *Increase your energy*. Go back to that chapter and look at what you are not yet doing that you can start to implement now. These are high priority areas for making the quality of your life the best it can be now.

Accept what you can't change
But what if there is nothing you can do to make certain elements of your life better right now?

There is an ancient Taoist parable that gives a new slant on how we should respond to events that are outside our control. It tells of an old man and his son who lived alone in poor conditions. Their only possession of value was a horse. One day, the horse ran away. The neighbours came by to offer sympathy, telling the old man how unlucky he was.

'How do you know?' asked the old man.

The following day the horse returned, bringing with it several wild horses, which the old man and his son locked inside their gate. This time the neighbours hurried over to congratulate the man on his good fortune.

'How do you know?' he asked.

The next thing that happened was that his son tried to ride one of the wild horses but fell off and broke his leg. The neighbours were quick to tell the old man that this was a disastrous turn of events.

'How do you know?' asked the old man.

Soon after, the army came through, pressganging young men into service to fight a battle far away. All the local young men were taken – except the old man's son, because his leg was broken.

As this story illustrates, it is often impossible to assess from our limited perspective whether an event is 'good' or 'bad'.

A lottery win might be perceived as great good fortune but it can be tragic for some people, breaking up relationships and causing great dissatisfaction.

Equally, something that might seem a disaster can prove in time to have been the best thing that could have happened. When I was in my 20s I was lucky enough to have a cushy part-time job which brought me in enough money to be able to support myself as a single mother. It came to an end abruptly, leaving me with no obvious way of supporting myself. I was devastated. I had been doing a little writing and had some pieces published. Now I put all my efforts into trying to build a writing and editing career, taking on everything I was offered and seeking more work. I had to accept projects where I had little expertise, which were enormously challenging for me – things I would never have dreamt of attempting when I had enough money coming in. The result was that I learnt very quickly and was put on course for the career I have now – something I might never have achieved if it hadn't been for my 'bad luck'.

What the story of the old man and his son also illustrates is that there is strength, peace and confidence to be found in simply accepting what is when you can't change it, instead of bemoaning or wishing it were different.

I am fully aware that this is easier said than done. It is most difficult when you are grieving. People in pain because a relationship has just finished, for instance, are desperate for the anguish to cease. Clients frequently ask me when the pain will end and how they can hasten the process. They want to find someone else to care about immediately but can't get interested, and find that people aren't interested in them as a partner.

It is unwelcome news that grieving takes the time it takes. There is a huge emotional adjustment to go through that is painful and can take many months. A relationship started too soon often goes wrong and can increase the suffering.

Accepting that this is the way it is means you can turn your attention elsewhere. When you stop putting energy into wishing things would change, worrying that they are not changing and cursing the unfairness of life for making you suffer, you can use your energy more appropriately. In the case of grieving, that would mean taking especially good care of yourself, looking for support from family, friends and professionals, and going back to basics again. Look for what you can be grateful for, and what small enjoyments and pleasures you can bring into your life now, and explore other areas in which you can improve your confidence.

You can also treat a bad event as a learning experience. I remember once reading an interview with a rich and successful man who was talking about a period of poverty in his youth. He said, 'If I'd known then that I was going to be rich now, I would have enjoyed the novelty and details of the experience rather than worrying about it.'

It is a bonus if you can enjoy the experience of accepting what is apparently negative. At the very least you can regard this as a time when you find out more about yourself and about life, a time when you can grow as a person, increasing your compassion for yourself and other people.

The Sedona Method – Letting go of control

The Sedona Method is a technique for allowing yourself to let go of wanting to control whatever is making you unhappy. Its essence is very simple: it involves locating the mechanism by which you hold on to negative feelings and simply allowing the feelings to float away. Although the theory (and eventually the practice) is simple, it can take time to find out how to do it for yourself. One way is to ask yourself mentally: 'Could I let this feeling go? Would I let this feeling go? When?'

There are books and tapes to help you learn the method. I can testify that it is remarkably effective on even the most apparently deep-rooted and painful of feelings. As Hale Dwoskin, the chief proponent of the Sedona Method says, 'When we want to change what is, we suffer. If you just let go of wanting to change what is as best you can, even for a moment, you are immediately happier. Plus, you no longer have to hold on to your problems in order to change them, and they often change or clear up all by themselves.'

Find whatever method works best for you by looking back at 'Putting worry into perspective' in Step 5: *Don't let fear get in your way.*

■ Match your goals and your attitude

Improving 'what is', certainly does not mean never setting yourself goals. On the contrary, having the right goals which really inspire you can be one of the things that light up your daily life, and make you accept whatever your current limitations are. Personally, I am happier not setting goals, but I recognize that many people positively enjoy them and I work with them to get the goals right.

The wrong goals are the ones that limit you and have failure built into them. Only one person at a time can be prime minister and there are many able, successful politicians who can never enjoy the fruits of their success because they missed the top prize. Wanting to be famous or nothing may leave you literally with nothing: no alternatives if you don't win that particular lottery.

Similarly, wanting it to happen right now may make the journey frustrating for you. Michael Neill talks about 'the pace of possibility', which he illuminates with two relevant quotes. The first, from Abraham Lincoln, is 'The best thing about the future is that it comes only one day at a time.' The second is from the Dalai Lama who, when asked how he saw the world in 50 years, replied, 'Madam, I don't even know what kind of tea I'll be having with dinner tonight. How could I possibly know what will happen 50 years from now?'

In one of his coaching tips Michael Neill writes: 'One of the questions I'm often asked by clients is how long I think it will be before they've successfully achieved the goals they come to coaching to pursue. I still sometimes make predictions, a sort of an "educated best-guess" based on what I've learned over working with people for the past 12 years, but I realize deep down there is only one real answer: as long as it takes – not a second more, and not a second less.'

TAKE ACTION: Michael Neill's project planner

Michael Neill suggests this six-point experiment:

1. Think of a project you are working on or planning.

2. What's the best-case scenario? How quickly could it get done? How little could it cost if everything works out just right?

3. What's the worst-case scenario? If everything that can go wrong does, how long will it take? How much will it cost?

4. What's the most likely scenario? If everything proceeds at the pace of possibility, what's the most likely time frame? What's the most likely cost?

5. What are your 'present moment power points' for keeping things on schedule and on budget? Which actions can you take in the moment to make the most difference to both the bottom line and the finish line?

6. Create a plan with time and money budgets that both hope for the best and prepare for the worst.

My own experience working with clients is that when your confidence is low, big exciting goals can actually be off-putting. Smaller goals that you can imagine yourself achieving are better. A baby goal, for tomorrow, once achieved, will increase your confidence to the degree that you can make a slightly bigger goal next time. If you are nervous socially, for instance, aiming to be the life and soul of the party may seem impossible, whereas finding one new person to talk to at a party is likely to be a more realistic challenge. What inevitably happens is that the scope of your goal will grow with your confidence.

Some people respond better to 'dreams' than 'goals'. Look back at the exercise 'What is your vision for the future?' in Step 4: *Be true to yourself*. The way to tell whether a dream or goal is right for you is to see the effect just thinking about it has on you. If it makes you feel weary and less confident then it doesn't serve you. If it excites you and makes you feel like taking action then you have found the answer.

Deborah – Choosing goals you enjoy

Deborah runs a successful small business. When she called in a consultant to talk about her plans for expansion over the next five years she was very impressed with him and his expertise. Everything he had suggested was so sensible. She had to work out the turnover she wanted to achieve in five years, and calculate what that would mean in terms of staffing levels, client base, premises, and so on. Then she had to work backwards. Where would she have to be in two years, then one year? Then what should she start doing now?

The trouble was that Deborah was totally uninspired by this, and she perceived this as being her fault. She couldn't get excited by the idea of the mega turnover she'd decided on. It all seemed to involve relentless hard work. I asked her to envision the way she would love her life to be in five years – not only at work but also outside of it. She wrote: 'The whole experience was a joy and although the outcome is only a list of things, I feel it is something that I can now build on. I feel how much bigger and better I will be for doing them! A huge step forward for a girl that never used to plan beyond today. This is such an enjoyable process for me!'

Enjoyment is the key to goals that not only draw you forward into a better life, but also help you to appreciate life as it is now.

Swap childhood labels for new adult beliefs.

Step 9
Let go of the past

❏ Acknowledge your childhood exeriences
❏ Hot buttons of vulnerability
❏ Shedding childhood labels
❏ How to confront the past

'The past is another country: they do things differently there.'

L.P. Hartley, The Go-Between

Who you are today is a product of all your experiences so far. All your feelings about yourself, including how confident you are, can be traced back to things that have happened to you or things that have been said to you, particularly when you were very young.

■ Childhood and the past

Childhood is about learning. Children are like sponges, soaking up everything they are taught, directly and indirectly, as they develop into the hugely complex being an adult is. Babies learn astonishingly fast. Things we take for granted, such as walking and talking, are immensely complicated, requiring a learning curve steeper than anything you will ever encounter again. As an adult the new things you learn will be much more simple; indeed, you may go many months without learning anything new at all.

By contrast, every waking minute in the life of a baby, infant or child is a learning experience: mud tastes horrible; smile and you get a smile back; banging your head hurts; smacking a drum results in praise, smacking a person results in shouting; 'please' is a magic word.

Children are driven and compelled to learn. You don't have to teach them to walk. They will work at it every waking minute, not put off by constant failure or by the pain of tumbles. They must and will master the skill, whatever it takes. Nobody has to remind them to practise how to talk. They will spend hours making noises, trying out ways of using their lips and tongues, delighting in using the words they acquire, and hungry to work out what the new ones mean, repeating them over and over till they are able to say them properly. All their apparently aimless playing and irritating mischief is actually about learning too; the world is their experimental laboratory.

Children are indiscriminate when learning. They accept the lessons at face value without judgment, adding another piece to the giant jigsaw they are building of the world, understanding how it operates and who they are in the scheme of things. They take as their guides the people around them, and the events that happen, and form their views and understanding on the basis of these, without question. These lessons go deep, and so they must. Putting your fingers in the fire will burn you. If you are to reach adulthood intact, you cannot afford to fail to learn the lessons of survival quickly and permanently.

Survival in the adult world also crucially involves how you interact with other people and what behaviour is appropriate, first of all so that you can be loved and protected, and then so that you can cooperate with and be accepted by others. Children absorb these lessons automatically according to the feedback they receive, and at a profound level they draw conclusions that they may never be able to put into words. From experience they simply 'know' something to be true.

It's unsurprising, therefore, that who we become has its roots in this learning; and because it is indiscriminate and unquestioning, some of what we have absorbed is unhelpful or just plain wrong. In therapy people usually discover that what is holding them back are the ideas, views and emotions that were formed at a very early age. Emotional pain, like physical pain, offers the most potent lesson: we want to avoid it. The way we decide to do this may turn out to be good for us – or bad.

For instance, a woman might seek therapy because she repeatedly has disastrous relationships with men. She is unable to trust them and her jealous behaviour drives them away. She discovers this is connected to the fact that her father died when she was two years old. At that age, all she could understand was that the man she loved had gone away and left her. The unconscious conclusions she drew were that you will be hurt badly if you love a man, because he will leave you. Although she can see as an adult that this is illogical, it has, none the less, shaped her world view at the most fundamental level and as a result helped determine her reactions to men.

These world views, set up as a pattern when you are very young, are consolidated as you grow older because you unconsciously seek out 'proof' that your instinctive feelings are right. You notice events and reactions that bear them out and add them to your mental files as evidence, even if you hardly know you are doing it. You naturally mistrust evidence that conflicts with these deeply rooted feelings and often reject it.

Social learning continues through later childhood and teenage years. These ages are characterized by a need to fit in and be accepted. Your view of whether the world is a hostile or welcoming place, and whether you are a worthwhile or unimportant member of it, has already been formed. How your peers react to you reinforces this and you modify your behaviour more consciously.

Oprah Winfrey – Take pride in your achievements

Oprah Winfrey, the internationally successful television personality, has written of her own experience of this. When she was in third grade at school she prepared a book report that so impressed her teacher she was praised in front of the entire class for it. Instead of this being a positive experience, it turned her classmates against her. She heard them whispering behind her back: 'She thinks she's so smart.'

This seemingly minor incident scarred her. Her biggest fear became that people would think she was arrogant, conceited and full of herself. She piled on weight – in some ways it was her apology to the world, a way of saying: 'See, I really don't think I'm better than you.'

It took many years for this view to change. Her television work, much of it focused on personal development and confidence, played its part. She says, 'I now understand that the true measure of womanhood is exactly what I'd avoided for so long – to be filled with all of who I am. Beginning when we are girls, most of us are taught to deflect praise.'

She believes it is a female trait to apologize continually for accomplishments and to play down successes. 'Every week I find my television studio filled with women who tell me they're so concerned with what others think that they've compromised their dreams and completely lost themselves.'

Oprah Winfrey has made it her mission to ensure that others are taught what she learnt the hard way – that taking pride in yourself and your abilities, and shining, is not only right but essential. That it took so long for her to get to that point shows the power that early messages have to dictate your life.

Early experiences determine what men and women think of themselves and how each of us feels we must be in order to be loved and accepted.

People with confidence issues have usually 'learnt' that they are not good enough in some way. To become a more confident person you need to exorcize the past – to hold these early lessons up to the light and examine them for holes – and determine to build a new and more positive world view. As Oprah's success has shown, this is perfectly possible once you become aware of the origins of what you are feeling and so are able to challenge them.

How 'hot buttons' affect confidence

Hot buttons are areas of vulnerability in you, where you are insecure, ready to be hurt and angry. Years ago the newspapers reported the story of a man who killed his wife because she moved the mustard pot from its usual place on the dining table. It was the last straw in a sequence of events that blew the lid off a pressure cooker of repressed rage. Few of us will commit murder but we all have hot buttons that, when pressed, will inexplicably unleash a raging demon, fill us with grief or keep us simmering with unexpressed anger.

Hot buttons are particularly relevant for your confidence. The origins of the hottest buttons are in childhood. You may think you have come to terms with what upset or frightened you, but underneath you are still sensitive to it. This sensitivity can affect your life. The child who lived in poverty becomes a multi-millionaire but continues to be driven by fear of destitution. If you were made to feel ugly, stupid, boring, unloved – or anything wounding – however resoundingly you have proved it to be false, the wrong comment can bring the misery flooding back. You might cover up the fact that you are alarmed or hurt, but your feelings will leak out as anger, a put-down or apparently arrogant boasting.

The origins of your hot buttons are often buried, which means that other people press them unwittingly. When someone's reaction is out of proportion to an innocent remark of yours, you can be sure you've pressed a hot button. I was having a pleasant evening with a friend when I remarked that I was disappointed she hadn't received the same benefit I had from some self-help tapes I'd lent her. Afterwards she seemed quiet and left early. She didn't call and didn't return my messages. Some weeks later she astounded me by saying how deeply hurt and angry she'd been but she now wanted to apologize because she'd realized it wasn't my fault. 'It was the word "disappointed",' she said. 'All my life I was told how disappointed my parents were in me. When you said you were disappointed I felt you were accusing me of failing with the tapes. To me it's the most cruel word in the world.'

■ Understanding your own 'hot buttons'

The areas of sensitivity created by the past won't go away overnight, and perhaps you'll always be more vulnerable to some kinds of behaviour or comments. This means that you have to let the people around you know what you can or cannot accept. Remember, just as you might unwittingly press someone else's hot button, others might do the same to you, unaware they are hurting you.

Instant cool-down

When someone presses one of your hot buttons and reactivates old feelings, don't attack, blame or suffer in silence. Let the person know how you feel: 'That's upset me', 'I'm feeling angry.' Give them the benefit of the doubt: 'I'm sure you didn't mean to hurt me.' If it's inappropriate to explain, say, 'I can't go into it now but I'm sensitive about . . . and I sometimes overreact.' Nine times out of ten the person will be sorry and want to reassure you.

Long-term cooling off

The exercises that follow will show you how to work out which hot buttons are connected to the events and the labels that wounded you when you were younger. This will alert you to where you remain vulnerable. Remind yourself that some people will press these buttons inadvertently, and work out your strategy: will you change the subject, stop them at once, or explain? Make sure the people close to you understand the no-go areas and why they matter, so that if they press a hot button you can remind them: 'I've asked you not to do/ say things like that because it brings up bad memories.'

Take some time to identify your hot buttons on page 235 of *Your workbook*.

■ Decoding childhood labels and messages

Most of our feelings about ourselves, and our hot buttons, are connected to the way we were labelled when we were young. What people said about you defined you, particularly if they were your family or people in authority, such as teachers. When you are little you don't have the experience or a strong enough sense of self to question whether the things that are said are true or not, even if you appear to. If your mother screams, 'You're a horrible, naughty little boy!'

you may stamp your foot and say 'No, I'm not!' but inside you grow to believe it. This powerful all-knowing figure has said it, so it must be true.

Similarly, children have no way of assessing the validity and reality of other messages they receive: 'I don't love you any more'; 'If you don't hurry up I'll leave you here and go home without you'; 'You'll be the death of me'; 'The monster will get you if you don't eat your peas', and so on. These are the kinds of things parents may say unwittingly, without any sense that there is anything wrong with them – they know they are not true. Children take these statements literally. If they hear a lot of messages like these they may not remember the words or individual occasions but will grow up anyway with a generalized sense that the world is an unkind or dangerous place.

Children also learn by watching. If Daddy shouts and Mummy is frightened: anger is harmful. Daddy rolls his eyes when Mummy talks: women aren't as good as men. Again, these lessons are so subtle that children grow up believing a whole set of things about life and themselves without being aware of where these notions have come from.

Labels are different, however, because you do remember how you were summed up by others when you were growing up, as surely as you remember your name. If you are constantly told that you are stupid, you will not only come to believe it, you will also make it true by not trying.

I know a very beautiful woman whose mother always told her she was ugly. To this day she still feels ugly, and thinks she's somehow playing a trick on people who tell her how lovely she is; a slightly critical remark about her looks or figure from an insensitive partner sends her into a spiral of self-doubt and a conviction that she is hideous.

Whole families of siblings are often assigned their roles – the good one, the brainy one, trouble, the charmer, the quiet one, the talkative one, the dependable one. The labels are rigid and unchanging, and can become self-fulfilling prophecies. Even the 'nice' labels can hold you back. Penny was known as 'the good one' at home and at school. She grew into an adult who felt duty-bound to be good all the time – to put others first, to work harder than anyone else and to ignore her own desires and inner promptings. Coaching was slow because she found it virtually impossible to separate what she really wanted from what she should want, and making time to improve the quality of her life was an alien concept that she found disturbing.

The way you were labelled when you were growing up always marks you in some way. For some people the labels become a spur, in an 'I'll show you' sort of way. My best friend at school was told she was no good at art. This angered her and gave her even more determination. She went on to become a potter whose works are collected by museums of modern art. More usually, however, the labels become a sentence you feel obliged to live out.

Refuting 'bad' labels

It's easy to see how negative labelling can affect your opinion of yourself. If the people around you think you are careless, scatterbrained, bad-tempered, disobedient, horrible, naughty, clumsy, a dope, or whatever it might be, it's hard to think highly of yourself. The tragedy is that these things are not true. All the above are features of childhood inexperience and growing-up behaviour. Of course, all parents will become exasperated from time to time, and all parents have to correct their children and teach them how to behave, but there is a world of difference between telling a child off for doing something wrong and telling them they are bad.

Imagine that you have wrongly entered the figures on a spreadsheet. You would probably accept your boss giving you a hard time over it. But if you are called 'stupid' and 'incompetent' you are likely to be rightfully angry. How dare they completely dismiss you and your intellect like this? You will probably feel defensive and uncooperative. Unfortunately, some of my clients work with people just like this, and I know these bosses never inspire their mutinous staff to do their best work.

If your boss treats you as an intelligent, well-meaning human being and makes sure you know why you went wrong, and how to put it right, your attitude will be very different. It's the same with children. If adults can demonstrate that they love and respect them, criticism can be a positive way of correcting their behaviour. But dismissing a child as 'wicked' or 'brainless' is damaging.

Coping with 'good' labels

It can be harder to see how apparently positive labels can be detrimental to you and your confidence. But, as with Penny, who was labelled 'the good one', these can also have unhelpful consequences.

In my favourite child-rearing book, *Between Parent and Child* by Haim G. Ginott, the author tells the story of a family car-ride. Two children are sitting in the back of the car, the baby strapped into a child-seat, the older child sitting unusually quietly and looking out of the window. The mother, wanting to reward him for his quiet behaviour, tells her older child what a good boy he is. Seconds later he takes the ashtray out and showers his parents with ash and cigarette butts. His mother cannot understand how her compliment could have provoked such a response. It turned out that the boy had been plotting how to kill the baby and that was why he had been so unusually quiet. When his mother told him he was 'good' the guilt he felt was so unbearable that he had to show her how bad he really was.

This story resonates with me because it makes sense of my own childhood reactions. I was a quiet, smiley little girl and people used to tell me how 'sweet' I was. Now there were times when I wasn't feeling sweet inside at all. I was sometimes having critical, angry or otherwise not nice thoughts. I never behaved like the little boy in this anecdote but the label 'sweet' made me feel bad.

I knew I wasn't really sweet but the label was like an instruction to be so. I reasoned that people liked me because they thought I was sweet, and so I was afraid that if they found out that I wasn't then they wouldn't like me any more. Indeed, although I hadn't started out pretending to be sweet, I was learning that I'd better keep up the act.

I wrote in Step 5: *Don't let fear get in your way* about the great fear of rejection I had for many years and how I needed everyone to like me, even if I disliked them, which led me to behave in ways that were not true to myself. After reading Ginott's book, I could see that this had been the result of my 'sweet' label.

You can see the workings of this 'good' labelling in adult life. Have you ever paid someone a compliment and found it backfired? When it doesn't go down well there can be a number of reactions, such as the perfunctory 'thank you' that doesn't sound very thankful, or the dismissive phrase, such as 'This old thing?' or 'Anyone could do that', and all the variations on the 'Yes, but . . .' theme: 'Yes, but so-and-so is much better than me', 'Yes, but it's not really very good, I have done better', 'Yes, but I'm so fat', and so on. If you truly meant your compliment and really wanted the other person to glow with pleasure it's disappointing.

Think of all the superlative compliments you have received. People say you're so brilliant, so nice, so good, so beautiful. You are pleased at first. Then, like the little boy sitting beside the baby in the car, there's almost certainly a corner of your mind that disagrees. You think of other people who are much more clever. You know that you're not nice all the time. You try to be good but you often aren't. You think you look all right but you are certainly not beautiful compared with . . .

What if the mother had told her little boy, 'It's nice that you're being so quiet, we're really enjoying the peace'? It is unlikely he would have reacted aggressively. Instead of focusing on his bad thoughts he might well have congratulated himself: 'I've pleased my parents. Maybe I'm not so bad after all.'

Compliments that concentrate on your own feelings about a person's skills or behaviour are much more likely to hit the spot. When you say, 'You're a genius with computers!' they think, 'No I'm not.' But when you say, 'I'm really impressed by the way you sorted out that bug in the program,' the other person is likely to deduce, 'Yes, I'm quite good when it come to computers!'

When you say, 'You're such a lovely person!' the other person may think, 'You obviously don't know me that well.' But when you say, 'It meant such a lot to me when you went out of your way to drive me home,' the other person may well react by thinking, 'I'm appreciated. It's nice to do things for people.' When you say, 'You're so helpful!' the other person might be thinking, 'I didn't want to help but I had no choice.' But if you say, 'It made a big difference to me that you did the washing-up,' the other person can reason, 'It was worth the effort then.'

Compliments that emphasize your appreciation of how the other person behaves always go down well: 'I'm impressed by . . .', 'I love it when . . .', 'I liked it when you . . .', 'You made me think when . . .' and then adding the specific action or personal quality that affected you so positively. Even 'I love you' can be improved when you start, 'What I love about you is . . .'

When a mother tells her son he is clever she will not necessarily boost his self-esteem if he knows that there are six children in his class who routinely do better than he does. But if she praises his behaviour – 'I was impressed by the way you came straight in and did your homework without being reminded' – he will feel good about himself.

I have worked with as many people who have been held back by 'good' labels as by 'bad' ones. And I find that unpicking the so-called positive tags always takes more time – the man who had been called 'a real boy' as a child grew up not knowing how to be gentle and emotional, and the woman who was the family 'beauty' always wondered if that was her only valuable quality.

■ Learning lessons from life

Sometimes it is the events in your life rather than labels or the behaviour of adults around you that have created your world view.

Jack – Reframing childhood trauma

Jack's lack of confidence stemmed from the great guilt he carried around with him. When he was six years old he was taken to his grandparents' house; he went reluctantly because it meant missing a birthday party he'd been invited to. Unknown to him, though, his grandfather was dying so this was intended to be a final visit. Jack was grumpy and uncooperative. He made a lot of noise bouncing his ball against the wall of the house when he was expressly forbidden to. His mother was inconsolably upset on the drive home and Jack believed he was the cause of her grief. The next day news came that his grandfather had died and Jack was sure it was his own bad and noisy behaviour that had killed him. As an adult he viewed the events differently and was able to understand the situation, but the belief in his badness had been ingrained in him for so long that he felt undeserving.

The lessons you draw from experience can be good as well as bad, of course. When she was ten Heather had an accident and she nearly died. This trauma could have made her fearful for the rest of her life, but it didn't. She became an extremely vibrant and confident adult. The message she had internalized was that life was unpredictable and could end at any time, so she wanted to wring the maximum from every moment of it.

TAKE ACTION: Confronting the messages from the past

What was said about you as a child? How were you labelled? What experiences have contributed to a negative view of life? Here are six steps towards understanding your past:

1 Make a list

Think back to your childhood. Can you remember being labelled when you were growing up? These might be clear labels, such as 'stupid', 'clumsy', 'good as gold', or they might be phrases in which there is an implicit label, like 'You never . . .' or 'Why can't you ever . . . ?' Or the label could be more subtle, maybe a particular 'look' that your mother would give you at certain times – no words were necessary to make you feel wrong, worthless and unloved. Remember to include the good labels as well as the bad. Most labels will come from your family and other significant adults such as neighbours and teachers, and maybe from teasing or bullying by other children.

When you have done this, list all the events in your life when you gathered messages that have made you feel not good enough and unconfident.

2 Consider the implications

Look at what you have written, remembering perhaps a typical occasion when you heard one of these assessments that has stayed with you. How did you feel about it when you were a child? How does it make you feel as you remember it?

3 Assess the label – how valid was it?

Take some time to think about the label or treatment you were given and ask yourself how fair it was. Perhaps you were very naughty, for instance, and you look back on how you were treated and think it was right. Think again. Were you actually evil? What else was happening in your life? What were you anxious or upset about? Remember that all children can be foolish, cruel and selfish at times. Judging your behaviour as a child by adult standards is wrong.

Perhaps it is more clearly obvious to you that the labels you were given were unfair, and also that the deductions you made were wrong. Acknowledging what was untrue and unfair starts the healing process.

Hilary – Cuddles and cruelty

Hilary thought she was a cruel and spiteful person. She wept when she told me how she had ill-treated her much-loved dog when she was a child. As she talked she revealed how deeply unhappy she had been at the time. Her parents were divorcing and there were constant frightening rows. She was scared and lonely, and she took it out on the dog. 'I wanted to cuddle him better,' she said. 'I would cry and cuddle him. I think it was the cuddle and reassurance I was yearning for myself.' With that realization she was able to forgive her young self and start the process of reassessing whether she really was a cruel and spiteful person.

4 Rewrite the past

How should the child you were have been treated and understood? If you were the other person in the situation, what would you say to your young self? How would you comfort and reassure yourself? What would be a kinder way of handling the situation?

See yourself as you were then. Then imagine yourself as both the adult you are now and the young you. Give yourself a cuddle. Say reassuring things. If you wish, imagine yourself standing up to whoever put the young you down. Give them a piece of your mind, whether it's a parent, a brother or sister, a teacher or another child. Champion yourself as you were then.

Do this even if you think you were wrong. Give your younger self a cuddle anyway. Say that you forgive yourself. Acknowledge you were only a child and you know better now.

If you find visualizing hard, you might want to write your younger self a letter from you now, saying the same kind of things.

5 How is the past affecting you now?

Look back at the areas of low confidence that you highlighted in the confidence quiz on page 15. Which can you directly relate to the messages from the past? Think of the ways you talk to yourself – when you tell yourself you are hopeless, unattractive, slow, weak or other negative things. Can you now see where these beliefs came from? Can you see that they were based on erroneous assumptions and unfair labelling?

For me, making the connection between the 'sweet' label and my excessive need to be liked no matter what, was a liberation. I could see that the label had created distorted thinking. I knew I wasn't sweet, but as a child I'd jumped straight to the assumption that therefore I must be the opposite and I had never examined the truth of this. I needed everyone to like me because I thought I was actually unlikeable. It didn't happen overnight but when I gave myself permission not to be sweet I discovered that I wasn't so bad after all. Yes, I could be sharp, irritable, grumpy or any manner of things other than sweet but most people still liked me anyway. I didn't suddenly become a monster, just more normal. I was able to be happier and more relaxed as I allowed myself to be who I am.

6 Forgive and move on

Most people are well meaning and do the best they can. Except in extremely rare instances you can be sure that no one set out to say or do things to make you feel so bad that you have carried the consequences into adulthood. If you are still very angry it can be hard to forgive, but until you can you are still giving them power over you.

It can help to write your feelings out in a letter. Be as angry as you like while you are writing it. The idea is not to deny your feelings, but to move on from them. You can write this letter even if the person in question is dead. Do not send it, even if the person is still alive. The purpose is to fully express your feelings, not to start a battle.

Then write a reply to your letter as if you were the person you sent it to. Don't strive to find positive things to say, just see what happens. You will surprise yourself by receiving an insight into what was going through their minds or happening in their lives.

Sam – Absent father

When Sam was nine his father walked out on the family and they never saw him again. As a result, Sam blamed his father for his unhappy childhood. He felt that he'd grown up without a role model to help him learn how to behave as a man. Living with a chronically depressed mother had made him hesitant and fearful, and he felt that he had never fulfilled his potential. When Sam tried the letter-writing exercise he was extremely moved by what he wrote from his father's point of view. He found himself saying that he missed his son, he was sorry that he hadn't been in touch, but he hadn't known how to handle the situation, and so on. Sam had no way of knowing whether this was 'true' but he had tapped into a healing vein of thought for himself.

Tom – Putting the past in perspective

Tom was equally able to move on after he wrote himself a letter from an unpleasant football coach who had made his early adolescence a misery. 'I never liked undersized clever boys like you,' he wrote. 'I couldn't be bothered. It was the big, athletic lads I cared about. I couldn't give a damn that you were upset by my treatment.' Although Tom felt his coach would never have said anything nice to him, he found the experience of expressing these nasty things extremely cathartic. 'He was a stupid man,' he said. 'I shouldn't have let him affect me for so long.'

Janet – Letters of compassion

Janet turned her letters to and from her abusive, long-dead grandfather into a correspondence that became an ongoing conversation. She also became inspired to find out more about his life, and felt able to ask other family members about him. This had been a taboo subject. 'I learnt about his war experiences, which were pretty horrendous. I began to see how he had become the embittered man I knew. In "his" letters to me, I found myself expressing his own sadness and disappointment with the way his life had gone, and this enabled me to have some compassion for him.' This took much of the sting out of her memories of her treatment at his hands. 'I realized that he was as much a victim as I was, and that helped me deal with the pain I had been carrying around for so long.'

Imagine yourself telling the person you exchanged letters with that you forgive them. If you can't feel it yet, try in a little while. Continue with the process of forgiving yourself and rewriting the past. Do the exercises in Step 10: *Choose to change your mind* – these will help you to change your view of yourself. As you consolidate your confidence and your feelings about yourself change, forgiveness will come more easily to you. Intermittently call to mind the people and the circumstances, and ask yourself, 'Can I forgive yet?' The day you say yes, you will be truly free.

Whatever you choose
to believe will become
your truth –
because you will look for
the proof that makes you
right.

Step 10
Choose to change your mind

❏ Change your negative thought patterns
❏ The power of personal beliefs
❏ It's never too late (to change your mind)
❏ Choose your new self-image

'The greatest discovery of my generation is that human beings can alter their lives by altering their attitudes of mind.'

William James

Most of us are unaware that there is a running commentary going on in our heads. How we see the world and react to events is coloured by the tone of this commentary. Some studies have suggested that on average 75 per cent of the thoughts we have are negative. Check your own thoughts. What are you thinking about your environment as you walk down the street? What about your family, your neighbours or the people at work? How are you reacting to the news, to the weather, to the state of your bank account? Most importantly, what are you thinking about yourself? Are you having affectionate, proud thoughts or are they exasperated, critical and unloving ones?

Negative thoughts do not produce happiness or positive experiences. Positive thoughts, on the other hand, do. Most people are intermittently aware of this but don't feel there is much they can do about it.

■ Recognizing negative thoughts

You can be having an apparently identical experience to someone else, yet your state of mind may dictate a different response. For instance, you are at a party with a gregarious friend who says afterwards what a fantastic occasion it was and how friendly the people were. But you weren't in a good mood; you were feeling awkward and unconfident, and found it an ordeal. You saw the people differently and perhaps you thought them shallow and pretentious, or censorious and uninterested in others.

You know, too, how your mood can affect the way you handle the circumstances of your life. You may have had a terrible day. You waited ages for the bus and then weren't allowed on. After weeks of not smoking you gave in and now you hate yourself. Your boss says if you're late again you're out. You battle your way through the rush-hour crowds to get home, and arrive feeling defeated and exhausted. The first thing your partner says as you walk through the door is, 'Let's go to the cinema and pick up a pizza.'

You're tired, fed up and worried about money, and this apparently pleasant suggestion seems presumptuous and selfish, so a vicious row develops.

Or you've had a wonderful day: a promotion and a bonus, you celebrated a colleague's birthday and laughed yourself silly. You went to the gym and the trainer said your improvement was astonishing. The first thing your partner says as you walk through the door is, 'I've spilt tea on the computer keyboard and it won't work.' This is going to cause you real problems, but your mood is so good that you can't remain cross. You see the funny side; it's not so terrible.

It's not hard to see how your feelings about life and yourself directly impact on your ability to cope. The more unhappy and conflicted you are, the more likely you are to be oversensitive and angry. When you're happy and at peace, goodwill gives you the strength, good humour and compassion to deal with even difficult circumstances.

Your underlying state of mind is most important in the way you see the world. When you are unconfident you are likely to experience it fearfully, angrily or with a sense of oppression or depression. You want something and are not getting it. From past experience, you expect disappointment. Life seems unfair. You have feelings of powerlessness or sadness. Your feelings about life, yourself and other people are negative.

By the time you have used some of the techniques in this book you will undoubtedly notice that as your confidence rises the world around you seems to change as well. As you feel better about yourself inside, the responses you receive appear different and events don't seem so threatening.

■ What the Thinker thinks the Prover proves

Many people have noted and examined how the way we feel affects our experience of the world. The Buddhist sage Nichiren Daishonin said, 'Heaven and Hell exist nowhere else but in our bodies.' The most succinct explanation comes from Robert Anton Wilson in his book *Prometheus Rising*. He suggests that our minds have two main elements: a Thinker and a Prover. The Thinker has theories about all sorts of things, and each of us has an individual Thinker. In the eponymous book of 1913, Pollyanna's Thinker thought there was something to be glad about in everything that happened in life, however grim. Grumpy TV character Victor Meldrew's Thinker believed the world was out to get him. The Prover, on the other hand, sets out to prove the truth of whatever your Thinker thinks. Pollyanna's Prover had no trouble noticing what there was to be glad about, which everyone else missed even when it was under their noses. Victor Meldrew's Prover, with his ironic cry of 'I don't believe it!', could all too easily find proof to support his idea that the world was hostile and dangerous.

If your Thinker thinks that only people with a string of qualifications can build successful careers, your Prover will gather evidence to show that it is true. However, if your Thinker thinks that talent and initiative are more important than education, your Prover will find compelling evidence to support this. More than that: your Prover seems wilfully to ignore evidence that is contrary to what the Thinker thinks, or at the very least not to notice or retain it. This is why people with different political views can look at the same set of facts and find the proof to substantiate their own beliefs, which might be completely opposed.

When you are unconfident it is because you have a set of beliefs that your Prover is searching for evidence to verify. You might believe that past a certain age you're unlikely to find love. You believe that only the grabbing and selfish get ahead in life. You believe that the world is prejudiced against people like you. Whatever you believe, you'll always find the proof that locks the belief in. In Step 9: *Let go of the past*, you will have identified which of these beliefs were given to you by your family and others. As you become more confident these beliefs are shaken and your Prover starts to see different evidence. New proofs are found to support the new you.

Fortunately, you can also start at the other end – see which of your beliefs are holding back your progress and decide to change them. This involves directly challenging your automatic Prover, and going out to look for proof that directly contradicts it. The evidence is there – you just have to look harder for it.

■ Changing your mind and finding new evidence

Positive thinking is so effective as a technique that it is the basis of cognitive therapy, which encourages people to look at their negative thought patterns and change them. It focuses on modifying a person's belief systems, expectations, assumptions and styles of thinking. A cognitive therapist can help you to become more objective by reminding you that your thoughts are only one view and not the same as reality.

Albert Ellis, a pioneer in cognitive therapy, developed what he called the A-B-C model.

- 'A' refers to an 'activating event' – an experience you have had. This experience will be described neutrally ('I was turned down for promotion').
- 'B' is a 'belief', and relates to how you have interpreted the event, and what you believe to be true about it ('Only the boss's cronies are promoted', 'I'm not management material', etc.).
- 'C' stands for the 'consequent emotion', which is how you feel as a result of your interpretation of the event ('I feel worthless, angry and resentful').

The theory is that it is your interpretation of an event that produces your feelings about it, not the event itself. Someone with a different interpretation will feel differently. A confident person who is turned down for promotion might believe, for instance, 'This company isn't right for me. I deserve better'. The consequent emotion becomes indignation, leading to an increase in self-worth, and the outcome might mean that the person will challenge the boss with extra reasoned arguments, or perhaps they will find the energy to go out and get a better job in a better company.

Consider this scenario: at a work meeting your boss slaps down an idea you have voiced. Here are some of the ways you might interpret it and the consequent emotions:

'I have terrible ideas.'
  Emotion = depression
'She's showing me up in front of the others.'
  Emotion = hostility and anger
'She wants to sack me.'
  Emotion = anxiety and panic
'That was rude but she's in a hurry.'
  Emotion = annoyance followed by acceptance

The last response is a balanced one. It is more objective than the others and the emotions are therefore less negative.

Cognitive therapy techniques aim to bring about more balanced thinking and therefore more positive and less unhealthy emotional responses. They are quite simple, but you will need to practise them regularly or your automatic thoughts and beliefs will send you back to the old patterns of thinking that have contributed to your lack of self-esteem in the past.

TAKE ACTION: Track and change your negative thinking

Become aware of what you are thinking and feeling by keeping a note of events and their impact on you. Think of an event to which you have had a negative response. It can be quite trivial for the purposes of this exercise. Here are four steps to get you started.

1 Describe the event in neutral language

'Partner reading the newspaper when I want to talk' is a neutral description of an event.

'Partner ignoring me as always' is a belief or automatic thought about the same event, and it is far from neutral.

2 Examine how the event makes you feel

What emotion does the event provoke? Make sure it is an emotion – 'I am upset' is a description of an emotion while 'X is ignoring me' is a belief or automatic thought, not an emotion.

How upset are you and how would you rate the intensity of your feelings on a scale of 1–10?

3 Think about your initial response to the event

Make a note of your initial interpretation of the event. What were your automatic thoughts and beliefs?

Something like, 'He's ignoring me', 'He doesn't care what I want', 'Our relationship is doomed', 'I'm boring', perhaps?

4 Consider whether there is another explanation for the event

Stand back from the situation and argue with your automatic thoughts. Are you assuming too much? What else might be true?

'He loves reading the paper', 'It's not a good time to talk', or 'He's tired and needs some time to himself', maybe?

It can be helpful to draw up a table for recording these incidents as soon as possible after they happen. This is one way:

1 Describe the event in neutral language	X didn't return my call
2 Examine how the event makes you feel	Anxiety (6)
3 Think about your initial response to the event	X doesn't want to talk to me. I do all the running in this relationship. No one cares about my feelings.
4 Consider whether there is another explanation for the event	X is busy. X never minds when calls aren't returned quickly. X is always friendly when we do speak.

1 Describe the event in neutral language	Memory of mistake at work
2 Examine how the event makes you feel	Depression (9)
3 Think about your initial response to the event	I'm so stupid. I'll never get anywhere. There's no point in trying. People are laughing at me.
4 Consider whether there is another explanation for the event	Other people I respect have made mistakes. There are ways to put it right. It's not a tragedy.

■ Identify self-limiting beliefs

In cognitive therapy you would continue making notes like this during the treatment, and work with your therapist to change your automatic thoughts and strengthen your logical thoughts. But for the purposes of this exercise, make detailed notes like this for a week and you will start to see a pattern. Many of your automatic thoughts will recur, triggered by a variety of activating events, and you are likely to notice that some emotions are more common – for instance, you may feel depressed more than you feel anxious or angry.

TAKE ACTION: How to choose a new perspective

It's time to look at what beliefs keep coming up, what your automatic thoughts are (your Prover finding the evidence) and what other evidence you can find to refute them. When you have done this you can start to modify your behaviour. You can do all this in eight stages.

1 List three beliefs that often occur in their various guises

These might be different words, depending on the event, with the same underlying belief: 'I'm unlovable; nobody likes me,' or 'I'm hopeless with people,' or, 'there's no respect these days; it's a dog-eat-dog world; if you're honest you get shafted.'

Writing these beliefs down is an interesting exercise in itself. Sometimes you can see that they are extreme and not entirely true. As you are changing with the work you are doing on your confidence you might recognize that these beliefs are old habitual ways of thinking that used to mean something but are no longer relevant.

2 What evidence do you have for these beliefs?

Your Prover will love this part of the exercise! You will probably find it fairly easy to list the evidence you have noticed to back these up.

3 What evidence do you have that contradicts this belief?

You might have to think harder, but you will probably be able to come up with some facts that say the opposite. Just one person who likes you, one example of goodness or an instance of a kind and honest person triumphing. However few, any contradictory facts are the start of the proof that your thinking and interpretations are somewhat distorted.

4 Build on this evidence

Start to search out more evidence for this contradictory belief. Don't judge or argue with the evidence, just note it. Helpful ways of thinking about this include asking yourself, 'What would X say about this?' Choose someone you admire, whose belief systems are different from your own. Also, 'What would I say to someone I cared about who thought this was true?'

5 Change your automatic thoughts

By now you should be questioning your beliefs and interpretations. Ask yourself how you could look at events so as to feel more confident and less cast down. Would this way be just as reasonable? Look at the automatic thoughts that often occur to you, and see if another way of thinking now starts to fit.

For instance, if your encounters with new people, and some of your past relationships, have led you to believe, 'I'm unlovable; nobody likes me,' or 'I'm hopeless with people,' this exercise will have brought some new ideas to your mind to balance the negative. A more realistic interpretation might be, 'I need to get to know someone before I can relax and make friends. Some of my relationships haven't worked out but there were good times as well as bad. I've learnt from them and I can take this learning into new relationships. Even the most lovable and attractive people have failed relationships. People can change or grow apart, or they may not be right for each other in the first place.'

And if your world view has been, 'There's no respect these days; it's a dog-eat-dog world; if you're honest you get shafted', you might be able to modify your view with the new evidence. For instance, 'I prefer to be around people who share my values of honesty, respect and fairness. Some people play dirty and I'm glad I'm not like them. I will be careful around those people and will seek out the others who are more like me.'

6 Choose new beliefs

Nancy Kline, in her book *Time to Think*, says:

We have to make a philosophical choice about what is and is not true about the nature of life and the nature of the human being. I chose a positive philosophical view of human nature and life. I chose it because it works. The human mind thinks for itself best when making a positive philosophical choice about the self and about how life works, when choosing to assume that humans by nature are inherently good, intelligent, powerful, full of choice, loving, lovable, able and alive.

I quite agree with her. What some people find hard to accept is the notion of choice in these beliefs. But as you've questioned your old beliefs you can start to see that there is a choice.

What would you like to be true? What would make your life better if you truly believed it? Write down three beliefs that, if you held them, would make you feel more confident and powerful. You don't have to believe them yet. How would you behave differently if you truly believed, 'I am a resourceful, intelligent person', or 'I can achieve anything I want', or 'I am lovable', or 'People are kind and loving when given the chance'? What would you need to believe in order to be able to express yourself fully and freely, and approach life fearlessly and with enthusiasm?

7 Assume these beliefs are true and look for the supporting evidence

Make a conscious effort to look for any evidence that supports these beliefs, and write down everything you discover.

8 Behave as if they are true

Behave as if these beliefs are true, as discussed in Step 7: *Act confident until you feel confident.* Jamie Smart writes in his newsletter of neurolinguistic programming (NLP) techniques:

I sometimes do a training exercise where I get people to shake hands with the other trainees a) while imagining that the person they are shaking hands with is going to be difficult to deal with, and then b) while imagining that the person they are shaking hands with is a great friend who will help them in many ways. The difference is always profound and it demonstrates (among other things) that what you are thinking changes the signals you give off. Someone once asked, 'So, are you suggesting we tell ourselves lies?' I replied: 'Not quite. I'm suggesting that you change the lousy lies you are telling yourself to good ones, which support you.'

What you will discover is that as you continue to behave as if you really do hold these beliefs, your Prover will gather more and more evidence that they are, in fact, true.

Beliefs for happiness on page 236 of *Your workbook* is a fun way to experiment with the power of trying on new beliefs.

■ Treat yourself with kindness

You are usually your harshest critic. In fact, most of us wouldn't stand being treated by others the way we treat ourselves. I tell my self-employed clients that they are the worst bosses they will ever have – unless they are prepared to make changes. Who could like a boss who takes work well done for granted and moans continually about shortcomings? Most of my self-employed clients do that to themselves. They expect to work days of a length that are positively illegal, and even nag themselves when they take a well-earned rest in the evenings. They berate themselves for laziness when they stop for a cup of coffee. They set themselves impossible targets and then beat themselves up for not meeting them.

Whether you are self-employed or not you probably treat yourself badly a lot of the time, in the way you think about yourself. People tell themselves they are too tall, too short, too fat, unlovable, worthless, a mess, stupid, too shy, too talkative, boring, not good enough. Not all the time, of course, but often enough to be damaging to their self-confidence. Only the most mean-minded people would say these things out loud to someone else, but thinking them about yourself is somehow considered modest or realistic. And what the Thinker thinks the Prover proves.

I was once very self-conscious about some rough areas of psoriasis on my feet. They disgusted me and I was sure they disgusted other people. Nevertheless, it was a very hot summer and I was wearing a pair of sandals, and my legs and feet were bare. There was a woman sitting opposite me on the tube and she became transfixed by my feet. She couldn't take her eyes off them and I saw the look of repugnance on her face. I cowered back miserably in my seat wishing I could hide my feet. Suddenly she leaned across and said to me, 'I've been wanting some sandals just like yours. Would you tell me where I could buy them?'

I was relieved and amused by my mistake. But if she had said nothing I would have 'proved' my belief that my feet were disgusting. Most of the time we're not so fortunate to receive such immediate positive feedback that our self-assessment is wrong.

■ What are you saying to yourself?

Start to notice the internal comments you make to yourself. You are likely to find there are a number of different 'characters' who say different things at different times. For instance, you might have a censorious judge who tells you that you are lazy or behaving badly, a rebel or defeatist who says you should give up because you'll never be able to succeed, a resentfully jealous person who compares you unfavourably with more attractive and successful people, and so on. Sometimes your self-talk will be nagging and critical, at other times it will be sorry for itself and crestfallen.

TAKE ACTION: Take the power out of negative self-talk

Here are three ways of challenging this unhelpful self-talk.

1 List the negative things you habitually say to yourself

Take some time to think about what these comments might be. Put yourself mentally in a situation where you know it happens. For instance, at a meeting there might be a voice saying, 'Don't say anything! Don't draw attention to yourself.' When you are getting ready for a party there might be a voice that says, 'You look awful, fat and old, nobody could fancy you.' When you're handed something new to do at work you might be telling yourself, 'Aaagh! I'll never be able to do this!'

2 Play with the voices

Imagine yourself in one of the situations you've chosen. Go over the phrase in your mind. Now say it out loud but change your voice. Try a goofy village idiot's voice. Then try a slow, sexy, drawling voice. Now try a squeak like someone who has just inhaled helium, then say it again with a giggle. Notice your response as you change your voice.

At a Tony Robbins workshop we were encouraged to say out loud our deepest, darkest fears about ourselves in the silliest voice we could manage while thumbing our nose and wiggling our fingers. It would have been the most embarrassing experience of my life, except that everyone else was doing it too. Even so, it was, of course, utterly ridiculous and childish. Nevertheless, it had the desired effect. Even today I can't think of the phrase I used to voice my fear without laughing at my stupidity. You will experience something like this when you realize that you can freely change your voice from its normal tone and pitch.

Experiment also with the volume of your voice. First of all make the voice very loud in your head. Now turn the volume down. You can do this by imagining a volume control knob, which you see yourself turning.

3 Ban the phrases

Now that you have recognized that saying these things to yourself affects your self-confidence negatively, and that you have control over how you talk to yourself, ban the negative phrases from your internal vocabulary. When one of them comes unbidden to your mind, turn the volume down or mentally say, 'Shhhh' to yourself, gently, until the voice stops.

■ Implant good messages

Good messages or affirmations are phrases that you say to yourself to bolster your self-esteem. If you tell yourself continually you are worthless, ugly or a hopeless case, your Prover will find the evidence to support this. Affirmations work in exactly the same way, so when you change the message to something positive and uplifting your feelings about yourself will improve, and your Prover will again find the evidence to endorse it. This process works faster if your body is tuned by excitement, exertion or fear – so if you repeat the affirmation while you are jumping on a mini-trampoline or when you are out jogging it will be especially effective.

Hazel – Raising self-esteem

Hazel took to this idea with great enthusiasm. Every morning before work she would jump on her trampoline saying, 'I am a fit, healthy woman who is superb at her job!' She found her self-esteem remained high throughout the day.

Some people will feel embarrassed about doing this sort of thing, but there are other ways of incorporating affirmations into your life. Changing your habits of thinking about yourself and the world really does 'change your mind'. Together with all the practical steps you are taking to build your confidence, the following five techniques will contribute to a lasting shift.

TAKE ACTION: The power of positive affirmations

1 Choose the best phrase for you

Look back at the list you made for choosing new beliefs. Is there anything else you would like to add? Is there a phrase that sums it all up for you, such as, 'I am confident and happy'? Choose one that you would like to embed in your consciousness. It is helpful to start the phrase with 'I am . . .' but if you feel a fraud saying this substitute something like, 'I allow myself to be . . .' Or you might want to start with something less personal, such as, 'I am going to enjoy whatever happens to me today.'

2 Repeat the phrase 20 times each morning

Like Hazel (above), you can go all the way and repeat your phrase out loud while you are being active or you might prefer to repeat it silently in your head. You can also write it down 20 times, like a pleasurable set of lines.

3 Say it with conviction

Make sure your tone of voice, either out loud or in your head, reflects the message of the phrase. If you are saying 'I am MD material' in an apologetic tone of voice it won't be so powerful – say it with strength and certainty. If you are affirming your sexiness, say it as if you mean it, as you would to a lover. If you are telling yourself you are going to enjoy your day, say it with vibrancy and relish.

4 Notice the results

Set yourself an experimental period – say a week – and see whether you feel any different. Remember that you have been saying the negative things for much longer, so it can take some time to make the shift.

5 Take the phrase out with you

As described in Step 7: *Act confident until you feel confident*, say the phrase to yourself at other times – for example, as you catch the eye of someone in the street, on your way to an interview or before making a presentation.

This would be an ideal time to review your scores on page 15, especially if you haven't done so for a while. If you have been working through the exercises, your feelings of confidence will have moved upwards to a more confident score. Congratulate yourself on how far you've come.

Has your attitude shifted in any of the areas? Has any of them become more or less important? Do you now feel ready to tackle something that previously daunted you? Building your confidence is a process that will continue. You will find that as your confidence grows you will ask more of yourself. And, as you do so, sometimes your confidence will drop again for a while. Your experience will tell you that this is a temporary matter – and you now know how you can build it up again.

The golden rule is always to look for the simplest actions you can take, and to monitor your energy levels. If your confidence drops it is usually because you are ignoring one of these basic elements. A period of paying attention to looking after yourself well and not expecting too much of yourself will restore the balance in your life and your emotional equilibrium.

The bonus in all of this is not only that you feel you can do more to be successful and fulfilled – and want to – but also that you are happier and more relaxed. A confident life is easier – not because you work less hard, but because without the old fears hard work is a pleasure rather than a slog.

In the words of Daisaku Ikeda, the leader of the Nichiren-based Buddhist organization the Soka Gakkai:

'The fight to create a new life is a truly wonderful thing. In it you find for the first time a wisdom that causes your intelligence to shine, the light of intuition that leads to an understanding of the universe, the strong will and determination that challenge all attacking evils, the compassion that enables you to take upon yourself the sorrows of others, the sense of fusion with that energy of compassion that gushes forth from the cosmic source of life and creates an ecstatic rhythm in the lives of all.'

23 short cuts to boost your confidence.

Confidence SOS: Your emergency toolbox

Sometimes you need a confidence boost right now. Although working through the 10-Step Plan is the best way to ensure a long-term revolution in your confidence levels, this confidence toolbox offers a series of techniques you can use at any time. The confidence toolbox should be used in conjunction with the 10 Steps, but many of the techniques can stand alone. Most are entirely new, but some are expanded versions of techniques already explained.

Some of the tips are simplicity itself to put into action. Some require more time. Some might seem bizarre. Sample the ones that appeal to you first.

Come back to any that puzzle you, or which seem odd, and decide to experiment. See what happens when you follow the instructions and you'll know if you want to use them again.

■ QUICK FIX

1 Look up

When you are feeling unconfident or depressed you instinctively look downwards towards the floor. An instant boost is to turn your eyes towards the ceiling and smile, whether you feel like smiling or not. You can also do this when you are walking along the street. Turning your gaze upwards will noticeably shift your mood.

2 Instant shoulder/neck relaxer

Imagine for a moment that you are carrying a ton weight on your shoulders. Now imagine it being removed and, as you do so, give a deep sigh of relief.

3 Confidence breathing

Confident, happy breathing is deep and slow. Hold your hand on your tummy and feel it expand as you breathe. Breathe in for a count of 5, hold for 20, and breathe out slowly to a count of 10. Repeat 10 times. You will feel energized, more confident and relaxed.

4 Becoming unstuck

When your motivation is low because you are feeling unconfident, you often grind to a halt and find it difficult to take any action at all. To break the stalemate, make a list of 20 daft but original ways to move forward. You will find that this shakes up your thinking and motivates you again.

5 Your magic words

These are words that help you to accept what is happening at any time, with an implication of positivity. They break through fear or cut into 'disaster' thinking. Choose a phrase that shifts your attitude at difficult moments. These are some phrases that help other people:

> Even this will pass away.
> Whatever happens, I'll handle it.
> One day I'll look back at this and laugh.
> It'll take the time it takes.
> The universe only sends you what you can handle.
> Everything happens for a good reason.
> What doesn't kill you makes you stronger.
> Where's the opportunity in this problem?
> I've handled worse before.

Do any of these resonate with you? Or do any that you've heard in the past? If not, make up a magic phrase of your own that has the power to invigorate you.

6 Look confident

Dress to express the person you want to be. Don't wait to be confident before you change your appearance. When your confidence is low, or you need it to be higher, dress and groom yourself with particular care. Choose a colour that you know suits you – doing this will lift your spirits even higher.

7 Relax at your desk

When you feel yourself tensing up at your desk, and your posture slumps, roll your shoulder blades backwards and forwards a few times. Then put the palms of your hands on the back of your neck and gently lean backwards. When you have done this, your shoulders will be down and relaxed, and you will naturally have a more confident stance, which will feed into your mood.

Check your posture and tension regularly and repeat the exercise whenever you notice you've gone back to bad habits.

8 Holding positive thoughts

If you have an ordeal such as an exam or an interview coming up you are likely to obsess about the difficulties that lie ahead, but this will only increase your tension and drain your confidence. This kind of last-minute obsessing never helps, so turn your mind to positive thoughts instead.

Think of those who love you

Call to mind the people (and animals) who have loved and valued you, including those who are no longer alive. Re-experience the deep pleasure that you have had in their company, and remind yourself how much more important these experiences and relationships are than anything you have to face.

Contemplate the difficult event

Continuing to feel the pleasure and self-esteem that come from these thoughts, turn your attention to what you are about to face. Notice how your priorities have shifted.

■ MOOD CHANGING

9 Change your state

You're aware of feeling unconfident and unresourceful. When this happens you need a technique to change your state to a confident one.

What is your current state?

Identify the state you're currently in. Become aware of how you are holding yourself, where you are tense or relaxed. What's going on in your mind? What are you thinking? What are you saying to yourself about yourself? Are any pictures flashing through your mind?

What do you want to be feeling?

How do you want to be feeling now? Happy? Confident? Relaxed? Remember a particular time when you were feeling like this. Recreate the occasion in your mind. See what you saw, remember the thoughts that contributed to your good feelings, the positive things you were thinking about yourself. Feel the changes that come about in your body as you relive the memory – how you straighten up, your muscles relax, the release of tension in your shoulders, hands, knees, and so on. When you are fully in the experience, feeling very different and positive, make an 'O' with your finger and thumb, squeezing them together, so that you associate how you are feeling now with that gesture and sensation.

Then change your mood by thinking of something completely different – what you had for breakfast yesterday, or a pink elephant with yellow spots. Then make the 'O' with your finger and thumb again, and squeeze gently to remind yourself of the positive state you were in a few moments ago. You will re-experience the thoughts, emotions and relaxation of that state.

10 Relaxation exercise

This exercise is for when you are lying down.

Think about your feet, flex your toes and hold your feet rigid for a couple of seconds, then let the muscles go, and feel the difference. Turn your attention to your calves and tense the muscles there, releasing them after a couple of seconds. Move up your legs repeating this, tensing and then relaxing the muscles. Your legs should feel heavy but relaxed after this. Now do the same with the muscles in your buttocks and groin, moving on to your stomach muscles. Turn your attention to your arms, starting with your hands and working upwards, clenching and relaxing the muscles until you reach your shoulders. Then move on to the muscles in your neck, jaw and face.

When you get to the end of this exercise, all the tension in your body will have floated away.

11 HeartMath Breathing

Doc Lew Childre set up the HeartMath Institute in California in 1991 to research the importance of the heart in well-being.

He found that the heart communicates with the brain and the rest of the body in several ways – neurologically, biophysically, hormonally and energetically. Scientific tests proved that activating loving feelings actually had a measurably positive effect on physical heart function, as well as on other organs, also reducing stress and causing an increase in confidence and well-being.

The institute developed a series of techniques to activate the power and wisdom of the heart. These techniques are now used in business, in the US military and in hospitals. One of these is a simple technique called the 'heart lock-in'. This involves finding a quiet place and time when you can fully relax. Sit comfortably and close your eyes.

Ignore the thoughts and concerns that are passing through your mind, and instead concentrate your attention on your heart. As you breathe, imagine that your breath is going through your heart. Breathe slowly and deeply.

Now think about someone or something you love, or call to mind something in your life you deeply appreciate. Continue to focus on this as you breathe into your heart for a few minutes. Pay attention to how this makes you feel.

Now imagine yourself sending that feeling of love and appreciation to yourself, and outwards to other people.

If your attention wanders, consciously bring it back to your breathing and your heart.

12 Make a confidence tape or CD

Music is an effective mood-changer, as you'll recognize when 'our song' comes on, or a song from your teenage years. Hearing the music puts you straight back into the state you were in when you used to listen to it, evoking the same emotions. It bypasses your conscious thought processes and acts directly on your mood and feelings. Identify which music or songs make you feel happy, excited, inspired or hopeful, especially those connected to occasions that bring back upbeat memories. Create a playlist or CD that has only these pieces on it. Play your personal selection any time you want to change your mood to one of positivity and confidence, such as before a party, a difficult day at work or an interview.

13 Create a confident environment

How you live is a reflection of your inner state. If your self-esteem is low, then you are likely to let things go at home. Stepping around clutter and putting up with dirt has a subtle, eroding effect on your confidence. Conversely, if your home is clean, tidy and welcoming it will have an uplifting effect on your feelings about yourself.

14 Use the power of scent

Your sense of smell is more important than you may realize. Like music, scent bypasses your thought processes and acts directly on your nervous system, triggering an immediate emotional reaction, good or bad, even if you don't consciously know why. Use scented candles or essential oils in a burner. Experiment with different scents to find out which one best helps your mood and confidence. Lavender is said to be relaxing; jasmine promotes confidence and strength; pepper, orange and lime energize, and peppermint is a wake-up call.

15 What can I learn from this?

When something goes wrong in your life, or you make an upsetting mistake, or even when a tragedy occurs, develop the habit of asking this question. This way you can turn any circumstance into an opportunity. Another question to ask is: 'If everything that happens to me is for my eventual good, what might be the meaning of this?'

16 Create confidence cues

To remind you that confidence is within your grasp, be on the lookout for quotations that make you feel good. Copy out your favourites.

Try writing the quotation on a postcard with a picture that makes you smile or feel good, and carry this around with you so that you can look at it regularly. Change the picture and the quote once a week.

17 Emotional Stress Release (ESR)

This is a simple physical technique that works quickly to reduce feelings of stress. Cup one hand and place it on your forehead, and cup the other at the base of your skull, resting the lower edge of the hand on the top of your neck, at the back. Hold this position gently for about three minutes. Focus on whatever issue is causing you stress. Concentrate on the main element of the problem and don't allow other thoughts to intrude.

You will find that your attitude changes. Things don't seem so stressful or you don't worry about them any more. The explanation for this is that making contact on the forehead and the back of the head brings blood to these areas. When you are stressed your body goes into crisis mode – ready to fight or run away – and for that reason blood flows to the muscles to prepare for action. To help this, blood is diverted away from the brain and the digestive system. The hand that rests on the forehead between the eyebrows and hairline makes contact with two points that are linked to the stomach by energy pathways running through the body. Touching them for a couple of minutes settles the stomach and brings blood to the frontal lobes of the brain. The other hand increases blood flow to the back brain (the more primitive area), and this speeds up the release of anxiety.

■ POWER PLOYS

18 Creating consequences

If you want to do something, or stop doing something, yet often fail, create negative consequences for yourself. I know one coach who runs workshops where biscuits are routinely set out for the participants at teatime; she offers £5 to anyone who catches her eating a biscuit, thus helping her keep to her diet.

19 Puncture bad memories

Does a specific memory from the past rise up on occasions to deflate your confidence? To banish this image you can change it to something that either inspires or amuses you.

Matt – Rewind, replay and reframe

Matt was haunted by a bad time he had as a teenager when he was bullied by a group of girls. Because they were girls he had no defence. He felt utterly humiliated.

Decades on, this memory would still rise up to make him feel weak and foolish, and was a constant reminder of failure as well as representing what he considered to be his fundamental lack of confidence. The picture of what had happened was as clear and bright in his mind now as then, and his hurt feelings were as acute as ever.

I suggested an experiment. I asked Matt to stand up, look towards the ceiling and replay the humiliating memory.

Then I asked him to rewind the memory and play the scene again, this time taking charge of what was happening and changing the outcome to one that empowered him. 'But can I do anything?' he asked. 'What I'd really like to do would be pretty awful!'

I told him not to censor himself but to do whatever he wished. He reported back that he'd tried a number of different scenarios, some violent and some superhero-silly. I encouraged Matt to 'play' the version that suited him best whenever the memory arose. But he never had to. He could now look back on the bullying and find it had lost its emotional charge – in fact his other versions made him smile whenever he thought about them.

Play back the memory
Stand and look towards the ceiling and see what you saw, feel what you felt, hear what you heard.

Change the script
In the same position, looking upwards, create a better scenario and outcome. Making it funny can be even more powerful than creating a realistic alternative.

20 Success strategy
The following preparation techniques are adapted from a tip by Michael Neill, and you can use them whenever you have an event coming up that makes you feel nervous, such as a job review, a meeting, a difficult phone call, an interview or a confrontation with someone.

Plan your strategy
Take some time to work out how you can best handle the event.

Rehearse your plan

Move through the steps and stages of your plan over and over in your mind. This will help you to relax and trust your body when the time comes.

Establish your intentions

Make a mini-checklist of things you want to do during the event or project. These can be both outcome-focused (get the job, have fun, be firm) and action-oriented (relax my body, choose my state, make a connection with each person in the room).

Play with possibilities

Now that you know what you want to do and how you want things to go, take some time to consider other options. What might go wrong? What might go more right than you expected? How else could you achieve your goal?

21 Preparing for a confrontation

When you have a difficult conversation coming up – making changes in your relationship with a loved one or asking your boss for concessions or more money, for instance – you can put yourself in the appropriate, unaggressive state by seeing the matter from the other person's point of view.

Graham – Changing perspective

Graham was full of complaints about his work, and his boss in particular. This man, he said, only cared about money – he was completely unreasonable in his demands, didn't listen and didn't care about his employees. Graham wanted to give in his notice, although he had no other job to go to. After he had complained to his satisfaction, I asked him to sit in another chair and pretend to be his boss. What was this man thinking and feeling? Incredibly, Graham's attitude shifted at once. He began to talk about the business from his boss's point of view: the company had lost a major customer and they were currently negotiating with a potential, but very difficult, new customer. 'He's very worked up about it, and what's going to happen to the company,' said Graham. That insight gave him a different perspective on the unreasonable demands that the boss appeared to be making on him. While still not liking the way he had been treated, Graham was able to sympathize with his boss's position. He then felt he should find a way of coping at work instead of leaving.

If you find yourself in a situation similar to Graham's, try this three-pronged approach.

Think about your side of the confrontation
What would you like to see happen or change in the other person?

Switch position
Move physically into another chair. Now put yourself in the shoes of the person you will be confronting. How would they see the situation? What outcome or changes would they wish to see? Notice the change in your own ideas as you experience the other person's point of view

Move into a third chair
See yourself as the arbiter. From what you've learnt, what advice would you give to yourself about handling the confrontation?

22 Be outrageous
This tip is adapted from a longer version by Jamie Smart, an NLP practitioner.

The 'pizza-walk' experience
One day I was on the tube in London on my way to train some telesales people, helping them to overcome sales-call reluctance (i.e. not wanting to pick up the phone and dial). I was reading the book *Change* (by Watzlawick, Weakland and Fisch) and came across a story describing how Watzlawick helped a student who had been unable to complete his thesis due to anxiety. He told the student, 'Go into three shops over the next week and make an absurd request.' The student did so, reported a shift in attitude and finished his thesis shortly thereafter.

I loved this idea, and thought it might be useful with the reluctant telesales team, but I knew that I couldn't ask them to do something I wasn't willing to do myself. As soon as I got off the tube, I went into a well-known hamburger joint outside the station. I joined the queue, looking around at the other customers. My heart was pounding like a drum; even though I knew rationally that I was in no danger, my neurology was responding as though I were about to hold up a bank.

When I got to the counter, I looked at the person behind it and, with a straight face, asked for a ham and pineapple pizza. She looked confused and said, 'What?'

I repeated my request. She said, 'We don't sell those.'

'This is a Chinese restaurant, isn't it?' I said. 'No,' she replied. I thanked her anyway and left. I felt like I had just knocked out Mike Tyson. I felt invincible!

Over the following few days I carried out several similar experiments. Each time my physical response was diminished, but in other areas of my life, the opposite happened. I started to exhibit less hesitation and more wanton go-for-it than ever before!

Thrilled with my success, I invited the telesales people to do similar absurd acts and they reported similar liberating results. I knew I was onto something.

Why does this work?

Our central nervous system is set up to protect us from dangerous situations. Many of us have been heavily conditioned against making mistakes (by teachers, parents, peers, etc.) and so we see them as dangerous. Yet making mistakes is an incredibly important part of learning, growing and exploring. The pizza-walk experience seems to help to eliminate this unhelpful response.

Try it for yourself, in the following four stages.

Identify your block

Think of the areas in your life where you hesitate and would like to just go for it.

Choose a venue

Walk into a public place, such as a shop, restaurant or petrol station, and make an absurd request (i.e. ask for something they definitely don't sell) while keeping a straight face. Be polite, safe and non-threatening.

Repeat the experience

Do the same thing at different venues at least twice more in the course of a week.

Look forward

Look forward to the situations where you would have hesitated in the past, and enjoy your new responses.

23 Find a confidence partner

One of the most powerful ways of making sure you do what you have decided to do is to involve someone else in the process. If you find it hard to get to the gym or go out for a run, for instance, join up with someone else. The thought of letting them down should be the spur you need to keep to your schedule. Similarly, a dieting partner – someone who shares all your successes and failures along the road to losing weight – will help to keep you on track.

As a coach I will give extra support if a client has something difficult to accomplish. For instance, I ask them to phone or email me after making each dreaded phone call, or to email me at the beginning of the day with a plan of action, following this up with updates at lunchtime and before the end of the day. Knowing that I'm expecting the report-back stiffens their resolve. You can devise a similar plan with a friend, colleague or member of your family.

An extension of this is what we call in coaching an 'integrity day'. I do this myself. I'll often partner up with another coach, setting aside a half or whole day to tackle something that we are both resisting. We call each other on the hour, every hour, taking it in turns to make the call. We spend two or three minutes describing what we want to achieve in the next hour, and how we managed during the previous hour, congratulating each other and commiserating with each other as appropriate. Even the most tricky things feel more doable when there's a friendly voice at the other end of the line.

Knowing that your own resolve and commitment is also helping your partner is part of what makes it so effective.

Taking action
changes you in
ways you can't
imagine.

Your workbook

'We must not, in trying to think about how we can make a big difference, ignore the small daily differences we can make, which, over time, add up to big differences that we often cannot foresee.'

Marian Wright Edelman

When I'm working with clients I soon know who is going to benefit most quickly from coaching. It's not the cleverest, the most talented, the one with fewest difficulties: it's the person who takes most action between our coaching calls. By action I mean what I've stressed time and again here: not grand, huge steps but lots of small apparently insignificant ones. However small the step, so long as it is followed by other small steps, it inevitably creates an unstoppable momentum.

These small steps, especially at the beginning, usually include a lot of thinking. It's our habitual thinking that keeps us stuck: 'If you do what you've always done, you'll get what you always got'. Fresh ways of looking at yourself, your life and your potential open up possibilities that seemed out of the question before. I offer unlimited email back-up between coaching calls, and when a new client starts bombarding me with daily, or even more frequent, emails, I'm delighted! This means that they are continuing to think, discover and do, well after the glow of our conversation has worn off. I know that very soon our coaching relationship will come to an end, as they will be flying solo.

In contrast, I have lively and intelligent conversations with some clients during which they are inspired and excited, but as soon as the telephone goes down they forget about it until the next call. They can make the changes they want in the end, so long as they stick at it, but it will take many more months.

It's the same with self-help books. I have a confession here: I've devoured dozens over the years, usually racing through them with great exhilaration, interest and pleasure. And then I've been disappointed: they don't work. More accurately, as I've come to realize, *I* don't work. It's easy to feel changed by an inspirational book, course or coaching call when in the middle of it, but unless the feelings and ideas are translated into action they eventually fade, and you are left exactly the same person as you were before.

When your confidence is the issue, it's part of the pattern not to try, or all too easy to feel that *you* are the problem. It's also easier to feel that actions won't achieve anything for *you*, because you believe you are a particularly bad case. It's a leap of faith to experiment with taking one small action, and then another small action, if you can't see how it will work. You'll only know whether it will or not by doing it anyway.

This is where *Your workbook* comes in. On the following pages are a number of practical exercises relating to the ten action chapters. These are designed for you to fill in as you go along, giving you an opportunity to reflect on what you've read and take action on it. Of course there are dozens of other exercises in the chapters themselves, which require you to find a fresh piece of paper or a notebook. Your excuse might be that you don't have one to hand. With the exercises in *Your workbook* there's no excuse!

I use the phrase 'commitment to yourself' a lot. You've made an important commitment to developing your confidence by buying and reading this book. Now you have the chance to make the changes you've committed to. Each small action effects a change in you, which makes the next action easier to take. Take the first action and you are on your way to being the person you want to be — the person you really are.

■ Using this workbook

Doing these exercises helps to embed what you are learning into your subconscious. Changes in your confidence are bound to follow.
These symbols show in what way the actions are helpful:

Success tip
A practical tip to further your success

Point to ponder
Something useful to think about

Attitude change
A fundamental change in your approach to yourself and life

IMMEDIATE ACTION PLAN

1. I want to improve my confidence in this area:

   Specifically I want to work on:

   I commit to taking this action:

2. I want to improve my confidence in this area:

   Specifically I want to work on:

   I commit to taking this action:

3. I want to improve my confidence in this area:

   Specifically I want to work on:

   I commit to taking this action:

 'Remember to choose the smallest, simplest, doable action'

MY ENERGY SECRETS

These are the things that make me feel good, and therefore more positive and energetic:

 'Recognize that treating yourself well is not an indulgence but a necessity for confident functioning.'

ZAPPING ENERGY DRAINS

On your lists of things that drain your energy there are probably items that crop up regularly, such as ironing or doing the accounts. Make a list of these and see if you can get rid of them by **DELEGATING** (asking someone else to do it), **OUTSOURCING** (paying someone else to do it), or **SWAPPING** (making an arrangement to do something for someone else in return for doing this).

ENERGY DRAIN	DELEGATE	OUTSOURCE	SWAP

'Finding creative ways to unburden yourself frees up energy for the important things in life.'

MY ENERGY-CREATING CHART

This is what I commit to do each day because it makes me feel good about myself.

Action	Mon	Tue	Wed	Thur	Fri	Sat	Sun

 'Choose daily actions that are simple to incorporate. Make sure at least two are purely pleasurable. Tick off each action as you do it, and feel your self-esteem rise.'

MY WEEKLY TREAT CHART

	TREAT	Day scheduled
Week one:		
Week two:		
Week three:		
Week four:		

'Treats don't have to cost much, if any, money. It's as important to clear some quality time for yourself and make arrangements to see somebody or do something to make yourself feel good. Planning for pleasure excites you about the future and is a sign that you value yourself.'

CONGRATULATE YOURSELF

List at least one thing you did today that you are pleased about. The more the better! Each day this week add at least one more.

Day 1

....

Day 2

....

Day 3

....

Day 4

....

Day 5

....

Day 6

....

Day 7

....

 'Concentrating on what you have achieved, rather than on what's missing, is a great new mental habit. How do you feel when you look back at this week?'

MY VISION

When I imagine my life in five years' time, this is how I'd like it to be:

'Allow yourself to dream. Don't think about what you'd have to do to achieve this. A strong vision has a mysterious power of its own.'

YOUR 'NO' LIST

What do you wish you could say 'no' to? Write your list here, and then tackle each item one at a time using the tips in *Be true to yourself*.

'Learning to say "no" gracefully is a powerful way to show yourself and others that you value your time and feelings. Notice how you feel when you've successfully refused to do something.'

FEAR MONITOR

My fear is:

Fear rating

low				medium					high
1	2	3	4	5	6	7	8	9	10

One action I will take towards solving it:

Fear rating afterwards

low				medium					high
1	2	3	4	5	6	7	8	9	10

'If the problem is out of your practical control you can choose actions such as talking to someone about it; doing something pleasurable from your *Energy secrets* list (page 224) to take your mind off it; writing without ceasing until you've said all you can about the fear; or tackle an energy drain that is within your control.'

LIFE-ENHANCING FRIENDS

Create a checklist of qualities you enjoy in people who make you feel good and positive about yourself and life in general.

'Think of the people you know: friends, family, colleagues and acquaintances, and see how they measure up against your checklist of ideal qualities. Plan to prioritize those who are most life-enhancing.'

THE CONFIDENT YOU

Choose the words you would like to be descriptions of you in the following situations:

WITH FRIENDS

'I am ....

....

AT WORK

'I am ....

....

WITH FAMILY

'I am ....

....

WITH NEW PEOPLE

'I am ....

....

 'Repeat these phrases silently to yourself just before the appropriate situation. Feel your body language change as you allow the words to change the way you experience yourself.'

GRATITUDE LOG

Today I am grateful for:

Day 1

Day 2

Day 3

Day 4

Day 5

Day 6

Day 7

 'Each day this week write down at least one thing you are grateful for — the more the merrier. Nothing is too small to log. Notice how recognizing the value of these things changes your attitude.'

IDENTIFY YOUR HOT BUTTONS

What are the things that people say or do that make you feel bad about yourself?

'I feel bad when people say...

'I feel bad when people do this around me...

'Knowing in advance what your areas of vulnerability are allows you to take charge of making changes. If someone often pushes one of your hot buttons, choose a calm moment to explain that this is hurtful so that they have the choice to respect your feelings.'

BELIEFS FOR HAPPINESS

Spend the week experimenting with a different positive belief each day, and then monitor how you feel at the end of the day

DAY 1 'Today I'll be working effectively.'

End of day rating

low					average				good
1	2	3	4	5	6	7	8	9	10

DAY 2 'Today my relationships will be enjoyable and positive.'

End of day rating

low					average				good
1	2	3	4	5	6	7	8	9	10

DAY 3 'Today I'll be living healthily.'

End of day rating

low					average				good
1	2	3	4	5	6	7	8	9	10

DAY 4 'Today I'm not going to worry.'

End of day rating

low					average				good
1	2	3	4	5	6	7	8	9	10

DAY 5 'Today I'll be at my most attractive.'

End of day rating

low					average				good
1	2	3	4	5	6	7	8	9	10

DAY 6 'Today will be different, not routine.'

End of day rating

low					average				good
1	2	3	4	5	6	7	8	9	10

DAY 7 'Today will be filled with fun and pleasure.'

End of day rating

low					average				good
1	2	3	4	5	6	7	8	9	10

'Try a new belief a day, just for fun. Five minutes before you get out bed (or while you are washing and cleaning your teeth) repeat the belief of the day and imagine what your day will be like if it is true. See yourself going through the day holding that belief: how you will behave, and how others will react to you.'

Further help

Books

Childre, Doc and Howard Martin *The HeartMath Solution* (Piatkus 1999)

Forster, Mark *Get Everything Done (and still have time to play)* (Help Yourself 2000)

Forster, Mark *How to Make Your Dreams Come True* (Help Yourself 2002)

Ginott, Haim G. *Between Parent and Child* (Pan 1967)

Gladwin, James *How to Live the Life You Love and Love the Life You Live* (Bene Factum Publishing 2000)

Harper, Robert and Albert Ellis *Guide to Rational Living* (Wilshire Bk Co LA 1975)

Jeffers, Susan *Feel the Fear and Do It Anyway* (Rider Paperback 1987)

Kline, Nancy *Time to Think – Listening to Ignite the Human Mind* (Ward Lock 2001)

Litvinoff, Sarah *The Relate Guide to Better Relationships* (Vermilion 1991)

Litvinoff, Sarah *The Relate Guide to Sex in Loving Relationships* (Vermilion 1992)

Litvinoff, Sarah *The Relate Guide to Starting Again* (Vermilion 1993)

Lowndes, Leil *How to Talk to Anyone* (McGraw Hill, 2003)

Norwood, Robin *Women Who Love Too Much* (Arrow 1986)

Watzlawick, Weakland and Fisch *Change* (WW Norton 1974)

Wilson, Robert Anton *Prometheus Rising* (New Falcon Productions 1993)

Websites

www.gethappier.com (for more information about Aboodi Shaby and his e-mail newsletter Get Happier!)

www.markforster.net (to receive Mark Forster's e-mail newsletter)

www.saladltd.co.uk (for Jamie Smart's NLP-based e-mail coaching newsletter)

www.sedonamethod.com (for information on the Sedona Method)

www.successmadefun.com (for details about Michael Neill's courses, tapes and e-mail coaching tips)

www.anthonyrobbins.com (for details of Anthony Robbins's courses and publications)

Addresses

The Society of Teachers of the Alexander Technique, 1st Floor, Linton House, 39–51 Highgate Road, London NW5 1RS. Tel: 0845 230 777828. Website: www.stat.org.uk

John Richard Laher (teacher of the Alexander Technique and grandnephew of F.M. Alexander), C28 Odham's Walk, Long Acre, London WC2 H9SA. Tel: 020 7836 7156

For information about life coaching over the telephone with Sarah Litvinoff go to my website: http: www.sarahlitvinoff.com

Acknowledgements

I would like to thank all my clients, who have been such a joy to work with and who have taught me so much, especially those whose disguised stories have been used here.

I'm eternally grateful for the wisdom, help, fun and inspiration of my two brilliant coaches – Madeleine Homan and Michele Lisenbury Christensen – and the support of the Euro-coach community.